D0995536

Growing
in
Health and Grace

Father Pat Collins C.M.

CAMPUS PUBLISHING

© Copyright Pat Collins C.M

First published November 1991
ISBN 1 873223 50 1

Design and Typesetting by Irish Typesetters, Galway
Printed in Ireland by The Leinster Leader.

Published by
Campus Publishing Limited
26 Tirellan Heights
Galway
Ireland

Contents

About The Author

Fr. Pat Collins is a Dubliner, the eldest of four children. He was ordained a Vincentian in 1971. Afterwards he taught for ten years in a secondary school in Armagh City. During that time he became involved with the charismatic and ecumenical movements in Northern Ireland. In 1987 he wrote about aspects of charismatic spirituality in a book entitled *Vi Daro un Cuore Nuovo* which was published in Italy. More recently he wrote *Maturing in the Spirit* which is a handbook for prayer groups.

During the early eighties he trained as a spiritual director at the Centre for Religious Development in Cambridge, Mass., in the USA. While in the U.S. he felt he was being called by God to "rebuild the walls of Jerusalem" (Ps. 51:18) by working with others to repair dangerous breaches in the life of the Christian community. Since then he has spent most of his time conducting parish renewal programmes and on-going formation courses for priests. Recently he contributed a chapter to a book entitled *Priestly Development in the Modern World*.

Over the years he has also become well known in Ireland as a broadcaster and writer on psycho-spiritual topics. Besides *Growing in Health and Grace* Fr. Pat has written another book on human development entitled *Intimacy and the Hungers of the Human Heart* (1991). Like many of his tapes it endeavours to help people to grow in loving relationships with themselves, others, nature and God. Currently Fr. Pat is a lecturer in spirituality and philosophy at All Hallows College in Dublin, and has been a guest lecturer on the subject of spiritual direction at the Institute of St. Anselm in the south of England.

Pat relaxes by spending most of his spare time with friends. He has a great liking for dining out, going to the Dublin and Wicklow mountains, attending concerts by the National Symphony Orchestra, browsing in bookshops, visiting electrical stores, travelling by motor-bike, drawing, listening to foreign stations on short-wave radio and tinkering with mechanical gadgets of all kinds.

Foreword

A few years ago I drove Cardinal Mc Cann to Cape Town to see the late Cardinal O Fiaich in Armagh. On our way back to Dublin, I discovered that the South African prelate had attended the whole of the Second Vatican Council.

After an animated discussion I asked: "What point impressed you most during the debates?"

He replied: "The universal call to holiness, the fact that it is not just for priests and nuns, it is for everybody."

Then he added: "By the way, if you ever write a book, don't forget to highlight the fact that all baptised people are called to holiness."

I don't know why it was—I had no idea of writing a book at the time—but those words made a deep impression on me. Since then I have given a lot of thought to both the meaning and the means of growing in holiness.

By the grace of God, I have been a Vincentian priest for twenty years, the last eight of which have been devoted to conducting parish missions around Ireland. During that time I have become increasingly convinced that playwright Eugene O Neill was correct when he wrote: "Man is born broken, he lives by mending, the grace of God is the glue." Yes, we *do* live in a valley of tears, there is a lot of suffering and unhappiness, but Jesus came to transform the situation.

"I have come to bring you life," he says, "that you may have it in abundance." (Jn. 10:10)

That is why he went about, as St. Peter testified, "doing good and healing all who were oppressed by the devil, for God was with him." (Acts 10:38) By freeing men and women from sin and the power of evil Jesus enabled them to become holy by growing in fellowship with God and loving relationship with others.

Except for the section, "Forgiveness and Healing", *Growing in Health and Grace* began life as a series of booklets. All sections of the book have three characteristics in common. Firstly, they are all inspired by the conviction that, in a qualified sense, *holiness is wholeness*. Secondly, each of them tries to interpret relevant psychological insights in a Christian way. Thirdly, there is a sustained effort throughout the book to be clear, concise, and practical. Its five chapters focus on two inter-related points. One concentrates on showing how a Christian can overcome common problems such as low self-esteem, resentment and unhealthy levels of stress, while the other focuses on how people can mature as Christians by means of dreams and friendships.

I want to thank Fr. Brian Doyle C.M. who first asked me to run courses on the subject matter of this work. I also owe a debt of gratitude to Fr. Brian Magee C.M. who encouraged me to express some of my ideas in print. I'm grateful to Fr. Martin Tierney of Veritas, for his kind permission to reproduce previously published material in this book. I hope it will enable you in some small way to become "holy as God is holy". (1 Pt. 1:16)

Pat Collins C.M.   **All Hallows College**
November 1991   **Dublin 9**

1
Forgiveness and Healing

We are all imperfect. So it is inevitable that we will hurt one another. The root cause is usually weakness rather than malice. Inadvertently we injure other people by word, deed and omission. We do this as a result of things like ignorance, insensitivity, lack of emotional self-control and the like. Unfortunately, there may be other occasions when we have to admit that, for some perverse reason, we deliberately set out to inflict suffering on another person. While we ourselves hurt others on a regular basis, we are more likely to be consciously aware of the hurts that they have inflicted on us. For this and other reasons we will focus our attention on the subjective experience of hurt and injury.

The Hurts of Childhood
Psychologists have shown that our problems begin early in life. Perhaps one or both of our parents were unable to give us the love we needed, because of things such as mental problems, alcoholism, ill-health, etc. As children we may have been the victims of unfair punishments, sexual abuse, destructive criticism, a broken marriage, etc. Ironically in the words of a Jim Reeves song, "You always hurt the one you love, The one you shouldn't hurt at all." It is often those who are nearest and dearest, such as family and friends, who wound us the most. The pain they may have inflicted can cause heartache down the years.

We may have suffered when we went to school. It could have been a bully whose verbal or physical attacks made our lives a misery. We may have been on the receiving end of the sarcastic and humiliating comments of an unhappy teacher. Counsellors, therapist and spiritual directors know that there is little or no truth in the proverb which says that "Sticks and stones may break my bones, but names will never hurt me." Normally, we forget the temporary sting of corporal punishment. Not so with repeated sarcasm and name-calling. Recently a teenager told me that, when he spoke up in class, his teacher retorted in front of all his fellow pupils : "What right have you to speak—your parents haven't even paid your school fees." Needless to say, the poor boy was mortified by this embarrassing and humiliating disclosure. A callous and uncalled-for response of this kind can bruise a person psychologically and undermine his or her self-confidence for a long time afterwards.

Adult Hurts

Unfortunately, hurt and injury are also common in adult life. People can say cruel and insensitive things to us. A fiancee can break off an engagement. A spouse can be unfaithful. A friend or confidant can betray our trust by revealing a secret, breaking a promise, or talking in a critical way behind our backs. A relative may try to cheat us of property or money. We can be the victims of things like violence, robbery, racial discrimination, religious prejudice, sexual exploitation, social injustice etc. The list of possible hurts is virtually endless.

Hurt and Anger

When we are hurt and injured by others we automatically feel anger welling up within. This God-given emotion is a healthy one, in so far as it provides us with the energy to defend our well-being and to fight against injustices. Speaking from a Christian point of view, St. Paul says (Eph. 3:26): "Even if you are angry, do not sin: never let the sun set on your anger." In other words, anger in itself is O.K.: it's the way you handle it that determines whether it is constructive or destructive. If you are involved in a hurtful conflict situation, feel angry—yes, but try there and then to resolve your negative feelings in a constructive way. Otherwise they can block your ability to either give or to receive love. There are two main ways in which this can happen.

Repressed Anger

Many people are reared in homes where all anger is considered to be sinful. It is true that Jesus condemned certain kinds of anger when he said (Mt. 5:21): "If you are angry with a brother or sister, you will be liable to judgment." What he was referring to here was the sort of hateful anger that can lead to violence and murder. The strong anger he himself displayed when he cast out the buyers and sellers from the temple (Mt. 21:12-14) indicated that he realised that a person could be angry, for example, about things like sacrilege or injustice, without sinning.

However, if parents disapprove of *all* anger, their children may learn to suppress this important emotion whenever they are hurt. A strong desire to retain the love and approval of their parents can motivate them to do so. As this type of repression is repeated, it becomes second nature. By the time they reach adulthood some of these people find it very hard to acknowledge any anger at all. They will have the *emotion* in their bodies—e.g. it will cause headaches, tummy upsets and stress—but they will fail to experience any *feeling of anger*. It has been buried alive in the unconscious. From there it can attack the person in two main ways.

Anxiety and Depression

Firstly, it can lead to feelings of anxiety. As self-esteem is lowered, feelings of worthlessness, helplessness, and insecurity seem to increase. Secondly, the extent to which negative feelings, such as hurt and anger, are repressed, is the extent to which one's capacity to experience positive feelings, like joy, enthusiasm, and loving empathy, will also be suppressed. The greater the hurt with its associated anger, and the longer it is denied at the level of conscious experience, the more likely it is that it will turn to depression. According to the World Health Organisation, "the blue plague" is the number one illness of the western world.

In my experience, a lot of depression is due to suppressed feelings of hurt and anger. It plunges its victim into a grey apathetic world devoid of positive feelings. It can result from a failure to carry out the advice of St. Paul, quoted above. There are others who, having being hurt in one way or another, do *feel* angry but, instead of resolving it immediately, they nurse their sense of injury and ire. As they do so, day after day, their anger festers until, imperceptibly, it turns into bitterness, antagonism, resentment and even hate.

Ten Symptoms of Unforgiveness

When the dynamic we have been describing becomes established, people enter a state of *Unforgiveness*. In other words, they are unable to love those who hurt them as they really are—imperfect sinners like themselves. Unforgiveness, therefore, is *a lack of unconditional acceptance*. It is more present in our lives than we are usually prepared to admit and can be discerned in the following attitudes and behaviours.

1. Repressed anger can be displaced into such things as anti-social behaviour e.g. arriving late for appointments, obstinacy, uncooperativeness, sarcasm, cynicism, harping criticism, judgmentalism, auto-eroticism, swearing etc.

2. If at all possible we desire to avoid the persons we resent. For example, we never visit a relative who was favoured at our expense in a will. If we happen to see him or her coming down the street we duck into a shop in order to avoid having to meet.

3. Sometimes the person we cannot accept—one's spouse or parent— lives in the same house as ourselves. It may be that we don't talk to each other for days or weeks on end or, if we do, there is no real meeting of minds or hearts. We avoid eye contact if we can. Otherwise we give the other person the frosty optic, hence the phrase, "If looks could kill."

4. People who bear a grudge tend to avoid any display of physical affection. If they do have to shake hands or embrace for appearance's sake, there is no warmth or spontaneity in their gestures. Unresolved hurts rob "love-making" of all genuine affection. A husband may force himself upon his spouse in a hurtful and demeaning way that can, in some instances, amount to a case of marital rape. For her part his wife may refuse her husband's desire for intercourse, by making some excuse or other.

5. Unforgiving people tend to overlook one another's good points while dwelling on and exaggerating their faults, real and imaginary. They do this in thought and conversation. If they hear the resented person's virtues, talents and achievements being praised in public they may have to reluctantly agree. Then after a mandatory pause they say, "I don't want to be critical...BUT!" Then they can proceed to an emotional assassination of the other person by drawing attention to faults and failures, both real and imaginary.

6. The state of unforgiveness gives rise to vengeful feelings, a desire to have other people suffer. As a result, we like to see them slip on the banana-skins of life. When we hear of their misfortunes we think to ourselves: "It serves them right, they had it coming to them, the so-and-so's".

7. Embittered people tend to project the responsibility for their own problems such as neuroses, lack of success in relationships, or alcoholism, on to other people e.g. parents or spouses. "It is all *your* fault," they commonly complain. "If only *you* treated me better I wouldn't be in this mess." By and large such people will fail to mature until they stop blaming others for their misfortunes and can accept responsibility for their own feelings, attitudes and behaviours.

8. Sometimes we will displace a sense of resentment on to an innocent victim. A man is humiliated at work. For one reason or another he is afraid to express his true feelings to the offender. But when he comes home he afflicts his wife and children with unreasonable demands, words and behaviour. I have noticed over the years that it's not uncommon for adults to project unresolved childhood feelings to resentment against parents onto anyone in authority, such as employers, counsellors and clergy.

9. Social prejudices are often rooted in a communal sense of resentment which is stimulated by a sense of shared injustice, hurt and discrimination. For example, many Nationalists in Northern Ireland share in a sense of resentment toward people and groups such as Ian Paisley, the Orange Order, members of the Ulster Defence Regiment, British soldiers, etc. In

recent years I have met a growing number of women who have an understandable chip on their shoulders about men in general. Because they may have been hurt or abused by a *few* men in their lives, they end up feeling antagonistic toward *all* men. Any form of feminism which is based on resentment is not genuinely Christian.

10. Some modern writers have pointed to a form of non-acceptance which is a type of envy. It is evoked in a person or group by the superior values and qualities of another person or group. It is a feeling of hostility, anger, and indignation which is neither acknowledged, repudiated nor directly expressed. It attacks the values and qualities that the "superior" person or group possesses, and which the inferior person or group not only lacks but feels unequal to acquiring. In effect it says, albeit at an unconscious level: "I can't forgive you for being superior to me and reminding me of my inferiority." It was probably this attitude that motivated the leaders of the people to seek the death of Jesus. In (Mk. 15:10) we read that Pilate realised "that it was out of *envy* that the chief priests handed him over". Over the years I have suspected that some of the people who work for justice on behalf of the poor are secretly motivated by a "feeling of envious inferiority". It is sometimes revealed in bitter and uncharitable antagonism towards the well-to-do.

Some Effects of Unforgiveness

The state of unforgiveness can have very negative effects.

1. Clearly, unforgiveness can ruin marriages, and divide families, communities and whole societies into different factions. One has only to think of the death and destruction in Northern Ireland and Yugoslavia to see the tragic effects of unresolved anger. As Jesus said (Mk. 3:25): "If a household is divided against itself, that household can never last."

2. Resentment can in some cases lead indirectly to emotional and physical illness. Whether conscious or unconscious, on-going feelings of hurt, anger and resentment can be very stressful. The true self is restricted, the psyche is disturbed, inner peace is forfeited. The resulting lack of harmony can interfere with the workings of the body's immune system. Research has shown how this can leave the person more vulnerable to

infections and diseases. For example, Dr. Ring of the University of Nebraska Medical School, asked his colleagues if they would send him four hundred patients whose ailments had already been diagnosed. He interviewed each person for fifteen minutes. Two observers ensured that Dr. Ring neither saw the patients, who were seated behind a screen, or asked them anything that might reveal their symptoms.

The doctor based his diagnoses entirely on responses to non-medical questions such as: "If you were sitting on a park-bench and a jogger came up to you and kicked you on the shin, how would you react?"

His success rate was impressive. He was correct about 100% of the hyperthyroids, 71% of the coronary occlusions and 83% of the rheumatoid arthritis. He was more than 60% correct in cases involving conditions such as asthma, diabetes, hypertension and ulcerative colitis. All in all, his first or second diagnosis was correct for 87% of the patients! Research results such as these, point to a clear psychosomatic connection between resentful anger and physical sickness.

3. Over the years I have noticed that in spite of their sins of weakness such as dishonesty and sexual irresponsibility, people can remain in spiritual contact with the Lord. However, the extent to which men and women let bitterness take hold of their hearts is the extent to which the life of the Spirit is quenched within them. It is not surprising, when one thinks about it. God is Love, unconditional and unrestricted mercy and compassion. The more resentment reigns in the heart, the more unlike God it becomes, until finally all genuine religious experience is obscured by the dark cloud of unforgiveness. Resentment against the neighbour we can see, is often accompanied, consciously or unconsciously by anger and resentment against the God we cannot see. The Lord may be blamed for failing to protect us from a painful hurt or injury, e.g. the killing of a relative by a drunken driver. Even if such people keep on going to church and praying, they may honour the Lord with their lips but their hearts will be far from him.

Forgiving Others and the Experience of Salvation

All of us are sinners. As the psalmist said (Ps. 130:3): "If you, O Lord, should mark our guilt who would survive?" If we had to face God's justice relying solely on our own merits and good works, the answer would be, no-one, because we would have to get 100% in the exam of life and, as we know from personal experience, that is quite impossible. But then the psalmist goes on to say reassuringly: "But with you is found forgiveness and for this we revere you."

For Those in Christ There is no Condemnation

This wonderful mercy, which eclipses the justice of God was manifested in a unique way by the death of Jesus on the cross. As St. Paul says (Rm. 5:8-9): "God proves His love for us in that while we were still sinners Christ died for us. Much more surely then, now that we have been justified by His blood, we will be saved through him from the wrath (i.e. the justice and punishments) of God."

In (Rm. 8:1) he adds triumphantly: "There is therefore no condemnation for those who are in Christ Jesus", i.e. all those who, by-passing the justice of God and reliance on their own merits or good actions, rely solely and entirely on the superabundant mercy of the Lord.

Over the years I have used a prayer exercise which aims to reveal my darkness and sinfulness to God, so that the Lord may reveal his merciful love to me. It is based on the language of the court, which St. Paul uses in Rm. 8. I imagine my whole life as being on trial before a jury. The prosecutor is the devil, "the accuser to the brethren"; my defence council is the Holy Spirit, "the Advocate", who pleads on my behalf. When I'm brought before the judge, he reads out the charges against me and asks: "How do you plead, guilty or not guilty?" "Guilty," I reply, knowing that it would be pointless to plead otherwise.

Then the prosecution begins to call a procession of witnesses, members of my family, friends, colleagues and people I have ministered to over the years. One by one they recount how I have failed them in love. My defence council asks them if they have anything good to say about me, and under cross-examination they admit that I have good points and that I display a charitable attitude on occasion.

Then the prosecutor says to the Judge: " My Lord, I ask your permission to show a video to the court. It contains evidence about the private thoughts and deeds of the accused." The video is shown. I blush with shame and the court gasps with shock as my innermost secrets are made known.

When the evidence is complete, the prosecutor makes an impressive speech. He points to the Christian ideals that I have professed over the years and then points to my obvious failure to live up to them. Turning to the jurors he says: "In justice, you should return a guilty verdict and call for the maximum punishment."

My defence council makes an equally impressive speech, full of compassion and understanding. While she has to admit that the evidence looks bad (I tend to see the Spirit in feminine terms), she asks the jurors to take account of my good intentions and the inner weakness I had to cope with over the years.

Then the judge asks the jurors to retire to consider their verdict. After five minutes they return to the court.

"Have you reached a verdict?" the judge asks the foreman.

"We have your honour." he replies.

"And how do you find, guilty or not guilty?

"Guilty on all counts," replies the foreman and, as he sits down, his fellow jurors nod in agreement.

The judge orders me to step forward. He asks me if I have anything to say. Dejectedly, I tell him that I haven't.

Then he says: " I have a few questions I want to ask your defence council before making a judgment and passing sentence. Does the accused believe that Jesus Christ is the divine Son of God?"

"Of course he does. He has his faults I know, but he firmly believes in the Lord."

Then the Judge asks a second question: " Does your client believe that Jesus died for the forgiveness of sins?"

"Yes, he believes that with all his heart. Every time he celebrates Mass, he is moved by the words of the consecration which proclaim, 'This is the new covenant in my blood which shall be shed for you, and for all, so that sins may be forgiven'."

"I'm glad to hear that,' replies the judge.

Then, after a solemn pause, he says: "I find the accused not guilty".

The prosecutor cries out: "My Lord, where is the justice in that decision? You know he is guilty."

The the judge says: "No. It is you who fail to understand. It is clear that the accused is in Christ by virtue of his baptism and his personal faith in the Lord. As a result, there is no condemnation for him, he is declared not guilty and acquitted. He can go free. There will be no record of the charges made against him!"

Be Merciful as God is Merciful

While we receive the grace of salvation in baptism, we only appropriate it in a personal fashion when we experience the mercy of God in such a way that we can accept that we are accepted by God and so can exclaim with St. Paul (Gal. 2:20): "I live by faith in the Son of God, who loved me and gave himself for me." This is *the* foundational Christian experience. It provides us both with the *desire* and the *power* to forgive and accept others as we have been forgiven and accepted. This is the first and primary response we can make to the gospel of God's merciful love, shown to us in the life and death of Christ. The Christian ethic, therefore, can be summed up in the words of Jesus (Lk. 6:36): "Be merciful as God is merciful."

The scriptures make this connection abundantly clear.

In (Sir 28:2 & 4) we read: "Forgive your neighbour the wrong he has done, and then your sins will be pardoned when you pray. If one has no mercy toward another like himself, can he then seek pardon for his own sins?"

This point of view is echoed repeatedly in the teaching of Jesus. In (Mt. 6:14) having told us to pray: "Forgive us our debts, as we also have forgiven our debtors," he says, "For if you forgive others their trespasses, your heavenly Father will also forgive you; but if you do not forgive others, neither will your Father forgive you your trespasses."

In (Lk. 6:36-39) Jesus says: "Do not judge and you will not be judged; do not condemn, and you will not be condemned. Forgive, and you will be forgiven...for the measure you give will be the measure you will get back."

The New Testament letters repeat this vital teaching. For example in (Col. 3:13) we read: "Bear with one another; forgive each other if one has a complaint against another. The Lord has forgiven you, you must do the same."

In (Eph. 3:32) St. Paul says: "Be generous to one another, sympathetic, forgiving each other as readily as God forgave you in Christ."

In (Jm. 2:13) we are warned: "For judgment will be without mercy to anyone who has shown no mercy; mercy triumphs over judgment."

Forgive and You Will be Forgiven

The extent to which we demand a retributive pound of flesh from the neighbour who has hurt or injured us, is the extent that we will fail to experience the mercy of God in this life and will have to face the retributive justice of the Lord on judgment day.

Conversely, the extent to which we are willing to forgive our neighbours from our hearts, over and over again (Mt. 18:21 & 35) in this life, is the extent to which the Holy Spirit will assure us inwardly that our sins are truly forgiven and forgotten (Heb. 8:12) and that we have nothing to fear on judgment day (1 Jn. 4:18). As Thomas Fuller reminds us: "The person who cannot forgive others breaks the bridge over which he or she must pass, for everyone has a need to be forgiven."

Motives for Forgiving Others

Only the Merciful Can Worship in Spirit and Truth

In (Mt. 5:23), Jesus says: "When you are offering your gift at the altar, if you remember that your brother or sister has something against you, leave your gift there before the altar and go; first be reconciled to your brother or sister, and come and offer your gift."

St. Paul makes a similar point when he says (1 Tim. 2:8): "I desire, then that in every place the people should pray, lifting up hands without anger."

A few years ago I was conducting a parish mission in the North of Ireland. When I went to the church, which was situated in a very Nationalist area, I noticed that there was a large inscription on the wall of a nearby primary school. It read: "Last supper for twelve in Newry." Immediately I realised that it was referring to the fact that the I.R.A. had murdered twelve members of the Royal Ulster Constabulary with mortar bombs as they were having a meal in the police barracks in the town of Newry. I was appalled and angered by this blasphemous linking of the Mass, which is a sacrament of forgiving love with a ruthless and cold-blooded murder. At first I thought to myself: "I'll have to mention this tonight." Then it occurred to me that many of the women present—it was the women's week—might be I.R.A. sympathisers. If they disagreed with any comment I made, they might not come back to the mission. I decided that, if I didn't want to empty the church, discretion would be the better part of valour. I resolved to keep my options to myself.

However, as I got near to the end of the service, I couldn't restrain myself any longer.

"I have seen awful graffiti on walls over the years, but the one on the school across the road is the worst I have ever seen. To rejoice in murder is dreadful but to link the taking of life with the Eucharist and the death of Jesus on Calvary is a disgrace, an affront to God and an outrageous blasphemy. If there are any of you who agree with me, you will do something about the situation!" The women listened in complete silence. I had no idea what they were thinking.

The next morning, as I approached the church at 6.15 a.m. for Mass I could hardly believe my eyes. The graffiti were gone. Evidently some women had sneaked out during the night and painted the whole wall, thereby obliterating the inscription. My heart rejoiced to think that there were people of such courage and Christian conviction in the parish. I really felt the worship we offered at the Eucharist that memorable morning was offered without anger in spirit and truth. (Incidentally, the numbers on the subsequent nights were as high if not higher than they were on the first night.)

Forgiveness and the Efficacy of Petitionary Prayer

All of us experience the need for God's help. We may have to ask him to heal a sick grandparent, to enable a neighbour to overcome a drink problem, to help a nephew to pass an exam, etc. It is encouraging to know that, again and again in the gospels, Jesus makes extraordinary promises about the efficacy of petitionary prayer. For example (Mk. 11:22-25) he says: "Have faith in God. Truly I tell you, if you say to this mountain, 'Be taken up and thrown into the sea,' and if you do not doubt in your heart, but believe that what you say will come to pass, it will be done for you. So I tell you, whatever you ask for in prayer, believe that you have received it, and it will be yours."

However, Jesus adds one proviso: "Whenever you stand praying, forgive, if you have anything against anyone, so that your Father in heaven may also forgive you your trespasses."

The implication is clear—We will only be sure about the promises of God when we feel inwardly united with the God of the promises. This rapport of faith is only possible to the extent that we appropriate the merciful love of God by offering it to those who have hurt and injured us. When we say: "Pray for us, O holy mother of God, that we may be made worthy of the promises of Christ," we are praying, among other things, for the grace of having a merciful heart.

A few years ago a Dutch priest who works in Ethiopia told me an interesting story in this connection. Apparently, when the members of one tribal group want to ask God for something, they come together in prayer. If they are at peace with their brothers and sisters they can put a stick on the ground. The villagers only make their request known to God when every adult is able to place his or her stick in the line. If a villager has fallen out with a neighbour the onus is on that person to forgive and to be reconciled. Otherwise the prayer cannot be offered. Surely this fits in with the teaching of Jesus (Mt. 18:19-20): "Truly I tell you, if two of you agree on earth about anything you ask, it will be done for you by my father in heaven. For where two or three are gathered together in my name, (i.e. in merciful love) I am there among them."

The Link Between Forgiveness and Different Forms of Healing

Unforgiven sin can be a barrier to the healing power of the Spirit. Jesus seemed to be implying this in the case of the paralytic. In (Mt. 9:2) he says to the afflicted man: "Take comfort, my child, your sins are forgiven."

When the Pharisees challenged him about his authority to forgive, he said: "Now which of these is easier to say, 'Your sins are forgiven,' or to say, 'Get up and walk'.

Then he said to the paralytic: "Get up, pick up your bed and go off home."

It is as if Jesus were saying: "Your spirit had to be healed of sin, before your body could be healed of disease."

The scriptures also make it clear that the power of healing can only be released in either mind or body, when we are willing to forgive our neighbours. A number of texts stress this point. We have already noted how the efficacy of all forms of petitionary prayer including requests for healing, depend on a willingness to forgive. (Sir. 28:3) is more specific: "Does anyone harbour anger against another, and expect healing from the Lord?"

Forgiveness the Key to Inner Healing

Nowadays countless numbers of people are looking for emotional and psychological healing. Experience has taught me that two things are vital if the desired inner healing is to occur. Firstly, we need to recover, name, own, understand and express our feelings of hurt and anger, either to another person, or to God in prayer. For more on this see chapter 3. Secondly, we need to move forward to forgive the person or persons, living or dead, who may have hurt us in the past, e.g. an alcoholic father or mother. As we forgive them with the help of God, agitation progressively gives way to peace, and hurt gives way to healing. I would have little hesitation in saying that a willingness to forgive is the key to inner healing.

Forgiveness and Physical Healing

We have already noted that some physical illnesses are psychosomatic in origin and may be the outcome of unresolved feeling of hurt, anger and bitterness. It sometimes happens, therefore, that as people experience inner healing as a result of forgiveness, their physical ailments are either lessened or cured altogether. Even in cases where the physical ailment is not psychosomatic in origin, forgiveness removes the main obstacle to the flow of healing power into our bodies.

A few years ago a young man in his twenties limped into the confession box during a mission. After giving him absolution I asked: "What happened to your leg?"

"I was knocked off my motor-bike two years ago by a motorist," he said. "My spine was injured, my leg was badly broken, and now it is shorter than the other."

"That must be difficult for you," I responded. "Did you get any financial compensation?"

"No!" snapped the young man angrily, "the driver perjured himself in court, he got off scot-free, and I got no compensation."

"So you suffered a double injury," I responded sympathetically. "How did you feel about the whole thing?"

The young man went on to tell me about his understandable anger and bitterness.

"The Lord has just forgiven you your sins," I said, "why not kneel before the statue of the Sacred Heart, look into his eyes and see if you can

20

continue to hold on to your resentment. If you are willing to forgive the man who injured you, ask the Lord for the grace to do so. He won't let you down."

I never met that penitent again. But some parishioners told me his story. He did what I asked, He knelt before the statue of the Lord, and asked him for the grace to forgive the man who had done him a double injury. It would appear that at that moment two miracles occurred. Firstly, the Holy Spirit descended on his will and enabled him to forgive as he himself had been forgiven. But at that same moment his spine and leg were healed and he walked out of the church without a limp. It was if the Father in heaven were saying: "If you forgive those who hurt you, you will receive graces in abundance even to the point of healing and miracles."

The Practice of Forgiveness

Over the years I have given many sermons on the need for mutual forgiveness. I have found that, as they listen, some people are acutely aware of the fact that they have been bearing a grudge against somebody or other. But many others say to themselves: "What he is saying is true, but it doesn't apply to me, I have no axe to grind with anyone."

This may well be true at the level of conscious awareness. But it would be naive to think that we have forgiven everyone who has ever hurt us. Often we repress or even forget a painful incident before resolving it through forgiveness, e.g. being sexually abused as a child. The painful memory sinks into the deeper mind, together with its associated feelings of anguish, shame, guilt, anger and bitterness.

In the 1950's a neurosurgeon called Wilder Penfield confirmed this fact. He discovered that, if he stimulated the temporal cortex of the brain with electrodes, patients could recall long-forgotten incidents together with the feelings they had about them at the time. In other words, we forget nothing. All of our memories are stored in astonishing detail in the unconscious. From there they continue to influence our conscious thoughts and attitudes with their negative emotional energy.

Remembering Unresolved Hurts
Recognising that this is so, it's a good idea to ask the Lord to help you to

remember if there is anyone from the past who still needs your forgiveness. On one occasion when I did this, I recalled an incident at school. I had been looking at a notice-board when a teacher told me to move away. Because I was slow to do so, he told me to go to his office. When he turned up, he made me bend over his desk and walloped me on the behind with a strap. I was seventeen or eighteen at the time. It wasn't the physical pain that upset me—I was used to that, we were often belted on the hands for all sorts of things—no, on that occasion I felt as if I had been violated as a person. I was angered by the incident but I felt such humiliation and shame that I never told anyone about it. As time went by I forgot about the whole thing. But when it all came back to mind a quarter of a century later I realised that the Spirit was prompting me to show mercy to this resented teacher whom I had never forgiven.

I have discovered that there are three possible attitudes to forgiveness.

• "I won't forgive."
• "I can't forgive."
• "I want to forgive with the help of God."

We will look at each in turn.

"I Won't forgive."

Many people have told me about their hurts and resentments during parish missions. Sometimes the suggestion that it might be a good thing to try to forgive the offender has evoked the sharp and adamant response: "No! Never! There is no question of it, not after what that person has done to me."

Once or twice I have been shocked by the sheer vehemence of such negative reactions. Invariably I'm saddened and disturbed by any unwillingness to forgive. If a man or woman refuses to extend mercy to another person, the Lord will refuse to extend his mercy to him or to her. It is a spine-chilling thought but, as long as they maintain this embittered posture, they are staring damnation in the face!

Most people fail to recognise that they are unwilling to forgive. At a fairly unconscious level the desire to be merciful is hedged around by all sorts of conditions such as, "I'll forgive you...if you change your behaviour e.g. stop drinking...if you give me what I want from you, e.g. your money, your appreciation, your love etc." In other words, a person may have the *wish* without having the *will* to forgive.

For many years I didn't get on too well with my mother. We often argued and hurt one another's feelings. I had made many attempts to improve the situation but without much success. In passing, I mentioned this to a woman I had met at a conference. Unbeknown to me, she was a skilled psychotherapist. After listening to my story for a while she said: "Let's do a role play. I'll be your mother. You can tell me what it's like to be my son." After some hesitation, I agreed.

Following a self-conscious start I soon got into my stride and poured out my hurts and complaints. Then the psychotherapist—she happened to be around my mother's age—said to me: "That was good. Now we will reverse the roles. I'll be you, and you will be your mother."

"No way," I quickly responded, "that's stupid, how could I be my mother?"

"Of course you could, you know her well. Now that I have listened to you for a while I'll be able to represent your point of view."

When I continued to refuse to reverse the roles, this perceptive woman said: "O.K., you don't want to go on with the role play. But I ask you to think about one thing. Why were you so reluctant to take your mother's part?"

Afterwards I did think about it. And then the penny dropped. I realised that, if for one moment I allowed myself to stand inside my mother's shoes to see and feel things for her point of view, I'd have to accept her as she was without any if's, but's, or maybe's as someone who had tried her best. Yes, I had *wished* to be on good terms with her. But my refusal to empathise with her was a subtle but disguised form of resentment, an *unwillingness* to accept her as she was. But once I allowed myself to see things from her point of view I discovered that I had both the desire and the power to forgive. As the saying goes, "To understand all, is to forgive all," and so, with Jesus, I was metaphorically able to say: "Father forgive her; she did not know what she was doing." (Lk. 23:34) After that, our relationship improved greatly. My mother felt freer to be herself, and I found that I was able to appreciate her goodness and love as never before.

"I Can't Forgive."

While many people would agree that it's good to forgive, and want to offer mercy to others, they end up saying: "I have tried, but I just don't seem to be able to forgive."

What they say is literally true from a purely human point of view. Remember the saying: "To err is human, to forgive divine." If we have been badly hurt, we will be unable to forgive without the help of the Holy Spirit. I have found that our wills are graced by two things above all else. Firstly, we need to recall and appreciate how Jesus has forgiven all our sins by his sacrificial death on the cross. What he asks in return is that we love one another as he has loved us, i.e. *by showing unconditional mercy*. Secondly, we need to ask the Holy Spirit for this grace which is so in accord with the will of God, while remembering the words of scripture: "This is the confidence we have in Him, that if we ask for anything according to His will He hears us. And if we know that He hears us in whatever we ask, we know that we have obtained the requests made of Him." (1 Jn. 5:14-15)

You could pray in these words or others like them:

> "Father in heaven, take away my heart of stone and give me a merciful heart like Yours. Forgive me for the many times I have hurt people. Help me, in my turn, to forgive those who have hurt me, so that we may be united in the power of Your love, through Jesus Christ Our Lord. Amen."

"I Want to Forgive With the Help of God."

Just as surely as the Holy Spirit comes down on the bread and wine during the consecration to transform them into the body and blood of Christ, so the same Spirit comes down on the will of a person who sincerely *wants* to forgive. It inaugurates a miracle of grace that progressively transforms desire into reality.

An Example of Forgiving Prayer

I have found the following method is effective in praying for forgiveness.

1. Close your eyes.
2. Imagine that the person who needs your forgiveness is standing in front of you.
3. See the person surrounded by the light of God's merciful love. Or see Jesus standing behind the person, his hands resting affectionately on his or her shoulders. Notice he looks at the person with the same love and mercy that he always extends to you.

4. Tell the person about the hurt or injury he or she has inflicted on you, together with its practical and emotional consequences.

5. Now say the following prayer, or something like it:

". . . (*Name the person*) in the name of Our Lord Jesus Christ, who loves us and who died for the forgiveness of our sins, I forgive you from the bottom of my heart for the hurt you have caused me, I release you, and call down the blessing and peace of God upon you and thank God that you are now forgiven. Amen."

The word *amen* means "let it be so, I believe it is accomplished". If we happen to meet the person we have forgiven, our feelings of hurt and resentment may begin to assert themselves again. It seems to me that it is important to affirm in faith that they have no real power. They are merely ghost-pains from the past. In reality, we stand in the grace and power of Christ's forgiveness. With his help we will be able to greet the other person, to look them in the eye and to talk to them without rancour.

It must be said, however, that some hurts go so deep that we can only forgive them in instalments. It is like peeling an onion. As soon as we have dealt with one layer of negative feeling, another one seems to surface to take its place. In cases like this we need to keep on forgiving until we feel that there is no resentment or bitterness left in the heart.

It is commonly said that we should forgive in this way and then forget the whole incident. Taken literally, this is psychological nonsense. How can a woman forget the fact that she was raped, or a man forget that he was kidnapped and tortured? No, we will never forget traumatic experiences of that kind. But as a result of forgiveness we can forget anger, rage and resentment, so to speak. They are replaced by a sense of inner healing, release, freedom, peace and good-will.

A few years ago I gave a talk to a number of travelling people about the importance of forgiving both the living and the dead. At one point I suggested that perhaps those of our relatives who are in purgatory may be unable to go to heaven until we forgive them. As Jesus said: "If you forgive the sins of any, they are forgiven them; if you retain the sins of any, they are retained." (Jn. 20:23)

It could be that our deceased parents and relatives reach out their hands towards us and sigh: "We know we hurt and injured you. In justice we deserve to suffer in this place. But in God's name, will you be merciful.

Forgive us, please, so that we may finally go to God and rest in peace."

A few days later a travelling woman called Julia came to see me.

She said: "Father, I was really struck by what you said about the souls in purgatory needing our forgiveness before they could rest in peace. My father and mother were alcoholics. They gave me a dog's life. I hated them, and felt nothing for them when they died. But when you said that they might be reaching from purgatory and pleading for my mercy, something melted in my heart. I went home to my caravan, knelt in front of a picture of the Sacred Heart, and told him that I wanted to forgive my parents for all the hurts they had caused me. As soon as I did, a wonderful feeling came over me. It was as if a heavy weight was lifted off my shoulders. I felt free inside myself. A great peace and joy came into me. To tell you the truth, I have never felt so happy in all my life."

Her radiant face confirmed the truth of what she was saying.

When I reflected some time later on her moving words I recalled a few lines from Shakespeare:

> *The quality of mercy is not strained,*
> *It droppeth as the gentle rain from heaven*
> *Upon the place beneath: it is twice blessed;*
> *It blesseth him that gives and him that takes.*
>
> *The Merchant of Venice, IV, i, 184*

2
Self-Esteem and the Love of God

A German priest was on the verge of a nervous breakdown. He went to Dr. Carl Jung for help.

"I can't cope with the pressures of a 14-hour day", he explained.

Following a long interview, Jung said: "if you want to recover, you will have to change your life-style. Work an eight-hour day. Have your evening meal. Then remain quietly on your own, until it is time to go to bed".

The priest expressed his gratitude: "I'll do anything you say, Doctor, if it will help me to feel better!"

The next day he worked for eight hours, had his supper and retired to his study. Soon he was restless, so he listened to some piano music by Chopin and finished a novel by Hermann Hesse. Next day he did much the same, only on this occasion he listened to Mozart and began a novel by Thomas Mann. At bed-time he felt as bad as ever. The following morning he returned to Dr. Jung.

"I carried out your instructions", he complained "but I feel no better."

Having heard how he had spent his time, Jung said to the unfortunate cleric: "You didn't understand. I didn't want you with Chopin or Hesse, Mozart or Mann. I wanted you to be all alone with yourself."

At this the priest said in alarm: "Oh! I can't think of any worse company."

To which Jung gave this classic reply: "And yet this is the self you inflict on other people 14 hours a day!"

The priest was a typical victim of what Mother Teresa of Calcutta calls "the famine of lovelessness". In the underdeveloped nations, she says, there is often a famine of the belly due to lack of food. In developed nations like ours, there is often a famine of the heart due to lack of love. As a result many people, like the German priest, suffer from a lack of self-esteem and peace of mind.

Psychology on the Importance of Self-Esteem

Psychologists differ on many points, yet they seem to agree about the importance of self-esteem. For example, Jung wrote these striking words in his book *Modern Man in Search of his Soul*.

> The acceptance of self is the essence of the moral problem and epitome of a whole outlook on life. That I feed the hungry, that I forgive and insult, that I love an enemy in the name of Christ— all these are undoubtedly great virtues. What I do unto the least of my brethren, that I do unto Christ. But what if I should discover that the least amongst them all, the poorest of all the beggars, the most impudent of all the offenders, the very enemy himself—that these are within me, and that I myself stand in need of the alms of my own kindness—that I myself am the enemy who must be loved—what then?

"Neurosis," he concludes, "is the state of being at war with oneself."

Surely, the priest who went to see Jung was neurotic in this sense. Rollo May, a well-known American psychologist has suggested that the civil war of the heart is diabolical. He doesn't mean this in a religious sense. He points out that the word "diabolical" in English comes form the Greek, meaning "to tear apart". So when a person who lacks self-acceptance is the victim of alienation and irrational inner conflicts, it is a "diabolical" experience from a psychological point of view.

Jung called the rejected, unaccepted side of the personality the shadow self. One image of the shadow is that of the retarded relative. Years ago families who were ashamed of a mentally handicapped son or daughter might lock the child in a back room out of sight. While that inhuman practice seems to be a thing of the past, we still do it to ourselves. Whenever the darker, weaker side of our nature is experienced, we reject it. Any feeling or desire that we find hard to face is hidden away, buried alive in the wells of the unconscious. From there, it poisons the waters of conscious feelings, thoughts and attitudes. The contents of the shadow can be brought into the light of consciousness in a number of ways.

Firstly, when the rational mind is off-guard during sleep, the shadow is revealed in symbolic fashion. It will become manifest in the guise of a figure of the same sex as the dreamer. In the case of a man it could be a pathetic, incompetent beggar he knows.

Secondly, we can project our shadow on to other people. We see and condemn in them what we may fail to see or accept in ourselves. This can be particularly true when we have a strong and irrational aversion to someone on television. Our prejudices can be given free reign at times like that. We can say what we like, because the people on the screen cannot be hurt by our remarks. However, it is the shadow that speaks.

Thirdly, relatives and close friends can be aware of the the shadow self. One of Shakespeare's characters says something like this: "The eye sees not itself, but by reflection. So I your mirror will reveal to you things about yourself that you are unaware of at the moment." (My paraphrase.) This encounter with the shadow is often the fruit of counselling, psycho-therapy and psychoanalysis. In each a trained person helps another to face and accept the truth about himself.

Growing Into Maturity

As a person moves away from neurosis, by integrating the shadow into conscious awareness, he grows into maturity. Psychologists suggest that such maturity consists of three inter-related elements.

Accept Yourself

While regretting my sins, I can learn to accept myself and my shadow. As St. Augustine said, we can hate the sin, and yet love the sinner.

As I learn to accept the enemy within, in a compassionate way, so will I learn to grow in self-esteem and a sense of bell-being.

Be Yourself

The extent of which I reject aspects of my personality is the extent to which I will hide my real self from others. I will only let them see those aspects of my life which I feel they might accept and like. As a result, I will end up hiding behind roles and masks. In biblical terms this is hypocrisy. The word itself comes from Greek. It has a theatrical background meaning "to act a part". It is only when I accept myself that I will be free to be my true self with others.

Forget Yourself

When the inner toothache of painful self-rejection is removed, then and only then will I feel free to pay undistracted attention to the experience of other people. This kind of empathy, unhindered by self-absorption, is love. As American psychologist Harry Sullivan has written: "When the satisfaction, security and development of another person becomes as significant as your own satisfaction, security and development, love exists."

Christianity on the Importance of Self-Esteem

Self-esteem is valued in both the Old and the New Testaments. In (Sir. 10:28) we read: "My child be modest in your self-esteem, and value yourself at your proper worth. Who can justify one who inflicts injuries on himself, or respect one who is full of self-contempt?"

This attitude finds an echo in the teaching of Jesus (Lk 10:27): "Love your neighbour as yourself."

St. Paul gives an amplified version (Rm. 13:9-10): "The commandments, 'Do not commit adultery; do not murder; do not steal; do not desire what belongs to someone else'; all these, and any other besides, are summed up in the one command, 'Love you neighbour as you love yourself'."

There is a fascinating meditation on this point in chapter two of St. Bernard's treatise *On Loving God*. In it, he maintains that our ability to love God depends on three things—dignity, knowledge and virtue.

Dignity

Bernard states that Christians have great dignity, or "inner glory", as he sometimes calls it. This is so for two main reasons. Firstly, we are created in God's image. Like him we are rational and free. Secondly, through the cleansing power of baptism we are united to Christ. As a result, the Father sees and loves in us what he sees and loves in his Son Jesus.

Knowledge

Bernard writes: "What glory is there in possessing something you do not know you possess?" Knowledge, in Bernard's use of the word, is not academic. It is the conscious awareness of our inner glory. However, he sees the danger of developing what is called a Pelagian point of view i.e. the mistaken belief that a person's goodness and worth come from himself and not as a grace from God. "We should therefore, fear that ignorance which gives us too low an opinion of ourselves," comments the saint, "but we should fear no less, but rather more, that which makes us think ourselves better than we are. This is what happens when we deceive ourselves into thinking that some good is in us of ourselves." This warning has great relevance where a good deal of humanist psychology is concerned e.g. the writings of men like Rogers, Fromm and Maslow. They do help men and women to appreciate their inner glory from a human point of view but they fail to appreciate the two main sources of our dignity mentioned above, and to acknowledge that our dignity is the gift of God.

Virtue

Bernard says that Christians have virtue when they consciously acknowledge that their worth is due to the grace of God. Surely this is the experiential root of all true religion. It is also the well-spring of sincere worship. When we appreciate our inner glory, we will begin to have a heartfelt awareness of God's glory. This sense of appreciation finds expression in thanksgiving, praise and adoration. Perhaps this is the reason why so many Christians no longer attend church, and why many of those who do, honour God with their lips only. Blind to their inner glory and suffering from low self-esteem, they cannot really experience, or respond to, the glory of God. As Bernard says: "Dignity without knowledge is unprofitable, without virtue it can be an obstacle.

Fifteen Signs and Effects of Low Self-Esteem

1. Feelings of Inferiority

A well-known Austrian psychologist, Alfred Adler, believed that everyone had to struggle to some extent with feelings of inferiority. Outwardly they might appear cool and calm, while inwardly feeling inadequate, shy, nervous and unable to assert themselves. He thought that such feelings could be lessened by the exercise of power and authority.

2. Morbid Guilt Feelings

We can begin to think that we are bad on account of the bad things we have done. People with low self-esteem not only hate their sins, they can come to hate themselves as sinners. As a result they feel unlovable in their own eyes or in the eyes of God. Needless to say, this attitude causes painful feelings of anxiety and guilt.

3. False Humility

Christian humility is an attractive and necessary virtue. But there is a counterfeit version. People with low self-esteem tend to overlook their talents, virtues, graces and achievements. They may believe because of their upbringing that such an attitude would lead to pride, the deadliest of sins. So they focus on their failures and weaknesses. Instead of leading to humility, this form of introspection can weaken self-esteem and lead to self-absorption.

4. Difficulties in Receiving Thanks or Praise

Appreciation is desired. But when it is received by a person with poor self-image, it is not really accepted or owned at the emotional level. Instead it is deflected. For example a woman who has been complimented for a lovely meal, responds: "Oh, it was nothing, I just threw it together", instead of saying "Thanks, I'm glad you liked it."

5. Difficulties in Receiving or Asking Help

Many people with low self-esteem appear to be very generous. They find it hard to say "no". Often their generosity is not as selfless as it appears. They may be motivated by a desire to please, a fear that unless they help, they will forfeit the good opinion of others. Implicit in this outlook is the feeling: "I'll only be liked for what I do, and not for who I am." When people like this need help themselves they are slow to ask for it. If they are offered assistance, they find it hard to accept. They say things such as this: "Really, it's OK, I can manage by myself." The sub-title here could read: "Don't bother with me, I'm not worth it."

6. Exaggerated Fear of Failure

Many of those who lack self-esteem are perfectionists. They feel, deep down, that they will win acceptance and love as a result of what they do well, rather than for who they are. Not surprisingly many of them are workaholics, prone to burn-out and haunted by a fear of failure of any kind.

7. Feelings of Jealousy and Envy

The insecure person becomes jealous when he feels that he cannot retain the affection of a friend in a three-way relationship. Tom likes Mary. Then Stephen comes along. He's handsome and charming. Mary likes him. Tom begins to feel jealous of Mary's relationship with Stephen because of his feelings of insecurity, rooted as they are in a poor self-esteem. The envious person is threatened by the gifts and achievements of another. In the light of that person's superiority, he feels inferior. This tendency to compare one's worth with that of others can lead not only to envy, but to antagonism and resentment as well.

8. A Tendency to Brag and to Boast

Some of those who lack self-esteem will tend to draw attention to their virtues and achievements in an off-putting way. The sub-title here could read: "I know you will only value me for my successes, so, just in case you haven't noticed, I'll tell you about them. Then you will like me." Sadly, boasting of this kind has the opposite effect. People react negatively, seeing the braggart as a vain and conceited person. As a result the poor self-image is reinforced.

9. A Tendency to Judge and Condemn Others

People with low self-esteem tend to be harsh on themselves as a result of their perfectionism. They will also tend to do to others what they have already done to themselves, i.e. to be critical and judgmental. They may try to disguise and control such negative attitudes with words like: "I don't want to be critical, but . . .", and then an emotional attack can take place.

10. Difficulties in Trusting Others

Clearly, if a person can't trust herself because of a rejected shadow, she will find it hard to trust others. This will be seen in relationships by an inability to reveal deeper thoughts and feelings. The reason? Fear of rejection. The sub-title here reads: "If you knew me as I really am, you wouldn't like me, so I'll only let you see that side of me that I think will be acceptable to you."

11. Sexual Difficulties of Different Kinds

Psychological research has indicated that very often people's sexual problems are rooted in anxiety rather than lust. The anxiety is the result of low self-esteem. As ego strength is lessened, instinctual needs are increased. The hope of erotic excitement promises to counteract the devitalising effects of on-going feelings of insecurity. However, if the person engages in erotic acts or fantasies that offend against conscience, temporary relief can be followed by an anxiety that is reinforced by guilt. And so a vicious circle is created, one that can lead to a great deal of unhappiness.

12. Addictions Can Be the Result of Low Self-Esteem

Many of the emotionally wounded live lives of quiet desperation. Not surprisingly some of them are tempted to engage in escapist activities that might deaden their inner pain. Unfortunately such people become addicted to cigarettes, alcohol, tranquillisers, sleeping pills, television, eating, gambling, drugs, etc. The distorting effects of these addictions can go on to increase a feeling of self-contempt. Again a vicious circle is created, in this case a dangerous and destructive one.

13. Negative Emotions and Aggressive Behaviour

This arises from insecurity and an inability to handle or acknowledge negative feelings like hurt or humiliation. People with low self-esteem often think of themselves as very sensitive. In a way they are. They tend to be very sensitive about the way others feel about them. They are not nearly so good at recognising what people feel about other things. Over-sensitivity can easily lead to hurt, the hurts to anger, the anger to bitter words and even violent actions.

14. A Tendency to Stress-related Illness

Negative feelings such as anxiety, hurt, anger, guilt, are stressful. If they are on-going, the body's defences are lowered and illness becomes likely. It has been estimated by the medical profession that at least 60% of all sickness and disease is due to this psychosomatic cause.

15. Negative-Images of God

What we think about God is often very different from what we may feel about him. Our ideas may be positive while our images of God may be negative and associated with negative feelings such as fear and distrust. People with poor self-image tend to project their negative attitudes on God, seeing Him as they see themselves, i.e. in a judgmental way. Not surprisingly, therefore, they feel a need to appease Him, especially if they suffer from morbid guilt. Unaware of their inner glory, they are blinded also to the glory of God.

Some Causes of Low Self-Esteem

In his poem, *In Memoriam*, Tennyson describes the way in which we develop a sense of self in childhood.

> *The baby new to earth and sky*
> *What time his tender palm is prest*
> *Against the circle of the breast*
> *Has never thought that 'This is I'*

> *But as he grows he gathers much*
> *And learns the use of 'I' and 'me'*
> *And finds 'I am not what I see*
> *And other than the things I touch'*
>
> *So rounds he to a separate mind*
> *From where clear memory may begin*

Psychologists say that early in its life a child experiences symbiotic union with the mother figure, i.e. a merging of identities. While being breast-fed satisfies his biological needs, the child is being fed emotionally and spiritually by the quality of the mother's love. The mother may speak, the baby may gurgle, but basically there is not an exchange of thoughts. Rather the child is enwombed psychologically, as his identity is established in the reflected light of the mother's love. The extent to which that love appears to be conditional or defective is the extent to which the child's sense of self will be weakened. We will go on to look at four different ways that this can happen.

1. The Problem of Separation

Sometimes a child gets the impression that it is not really very lovable, because of being separated from its parents, especially the mother. There can be many reasons for this. Firstly, the child may be born prematurely. As a result it is kept in a hospital incubator, and so deprived of physical contact with the parents. Or it may be that the child may have to go to hospital in its first few years. The parents visit, then they go away again. The child can feel rejected. If it does, it blames itself. If feels: "There must be something wrong with me, that is why my parents keep on leaving me!" Secondly, it may be that the mother has to go to hospital for an extended period. She might even die. The child doesn't understand this. It feels deserted and abandoned. As a result it suffers from what psychologists call separation anxiety, a feeling that can keep on re-surfacing in adult life. Thirdly, sometimes a sick or pregnant mother will send one of her children to stay with a grandmother or aunt. This may lead to the child being brought up by the relative. In some cases the child may get the mistaken impression that it was given away, because it wasn't wanted, which can have a detrimental effect on self-esteem.

2. Lack of Affection

For one reason or another, parents may be unable to give a child the love it needs. If either is suffering from emotional problems, e.g. depression, he or she won't have the ability to give the child enough affection. Sometimes a mother's energies are absorbed with the difficult task of coping with an alcoholic husband. Worry about bills and possible violence creates an atmosphere of tension and fear. This kind of environment generates anxiety not self-esteem. Lastly, some couples have more children than they can really care for. As a result one or more of them may feel neglected from an emotional point of view. Even in smaller families, children can feel much the same, because their parents are unable to express physical affection to them or to one another, or to say the words, "I love you."

3. Conditional Love

A child is a bundle of selfish needs and desires. Naturally the parents try to fit it into the life of the family and to prevent it causing damage or disruption. Sometimes in the course of disciplining the child, the parents can give the impression that their love is conditional. It depends on the child's willingness to do as he is told. Their words, tone of voice and facial features can say to the child: "I'll love you more if . . . if you do as you are told . . . if you don't go into temper tantrums, etc." In the child's mind this can give rise to the belief that "I'm lovable for what I do, and not for who I am." This kind of conclusion damages self-esteem. In adult life it expresses itself in perfectionism, fear of failure and morbid guilt, as we have seen above.

4. Lack of Affirmation

When I was a teacher I used to bring a large sheet of white paper into class. I'd hold it up and ask: "Well boys, what do you see?"

"White paper, Father", they would reply.

Then I'd open my fountain pen and flick it in the direction of the paper so that a blob of ink would splash on to the surface.

"What doe you see now?" I'd ask.

"A blue blob on white paper", the boys would reply in a chorus of voices.

"Are you sure?"

"Yes, Father."

Then I'd look at the sheet and say: "What I see is a white sheet with a blue blob on it", indicating that at least 95% of the surface was still white.

Many parents and teachers are too critical of their children. They are inclined to see the blobs, to find fault and to expect the worst, while neglecting to show appreciation, and confident expectation. As a result, self-esteem is damaged and the child fails to develop his potential. The same kind of thing can go on in adult life. A person's best efforts are taken for granted, but as soon as he makes a mistake he hears all about it. The effect is not only discouraging, it also reinforces a bad self-image.

How to Grow in Self-Esteem

The late Carl Rogers has had a great influence on the theory and practice of counselling. He believed that no matter what a person's presenting problem might be, e.g. panic attacks, kleptomania, sexual impotence, etc., the root cause was usually the same, namely, lack of self-acceptance. As a result he felt that the key to effective therapy was to listen with a kind of empathy that would enter into the experience of the other person without judgment or directives. To offer unconditional acceptance in this way helps the sufferer to grow in self-acceptance. This in turn provides him with the desire and the power to change his life in accord with his beliefs and values. This is a very Christian approach, one that has many implications for our subject.

1. Self-Disclosure
We have seen that lack of self-esteem can be due to a lack of unconditional love. So the way to healing is to feel accepted and loved as you are now, without condition. This insight lies behind the fifth step of Alcoholics Anonymous. Having made a fearless examination of conscience, the recovering alcoholic is encouraged to reveal his dark secrets to another human being. Sometimes it takes years before the AA member has the courage to take this step. I have been deeply moved by the honesty of alcoholics as they struggled with a mixture of conviction and fear to tell me about the shadow side of their lives. I could see that they were afraid that I would be shocked or disgusted by what they said. Their fear that I would reject them mirrored their own attitude to themselves, the very

lack of self-esteem that may have led them to drink in the first place. But when they found that they were accepted, loved and appreciated as they were, and not as they had pretended to be, a great healing took place. They learned to accept and love the enemy within.

Whether we have a drink problem or not, we can all learn from the members of AA. Our self-image will be improved when we can tell another human being about our real selves, about our failures, secrets and fears. We can talk to a trusted friend or confidant such as a priest or a counsellor.

I did this one New Year's Day when I was with a friend. I found myself telling him things I had never told anyone before. About half way through I thought: "What am I doing? Perhaps I should stop now." But something within told me to go for broke. In my mind I knew there was no likelihood of rejection. In my heart I feared it strongly. Well, I told my whole story. it was met with empathy, understanding, acceptance and affection. In the light of that acceptance and love, I began to accept and love myself in a new way. It was a real experience of healing. I was reminded of two scripture texts: "If you forgive people's sins, they are forgiven" (Jn. 20:23), and "Confess your sins to one another, so that you will be healed" (Jm. 5:16).

2. *Prayer for Inner Healing*

Self-disclosure isn't always enough. Some emotional hurts go so deep that they may need the kind of inner healing that comes as a result of prayer.

If that is the case, the following may help:

• Recall the painful memory or hurt that needs a healing touch.
• Consider these words about the passion of Jesus: "By his wounds our wounds are being healed" (Is. 53:5).
• Tell the Lord about your feelings and offer your hurt to him.
• Ask the Lord to heal you with the kind of faith that *expects* results, knowing that "nothing is impossible to God" (Lk. 1:37) and that "whatever you ask for believing you have received, it will be yours" (Mk. 11:24).
• Thank God for the inner healing He has already begun in your life.

If possible, it can be very helpful to go to another Christian who is experienced in the area of prayer for inner healing. People with this talent from God often have a gift of discernment, i.e. an ability to discover the root cause of a hurt. They may do this by asking questions or occasionally by a divinely inspired intuition. I know a priest who saw a man who was suffering from chronic claustrophobia. He had been to two psychiatrists without success. After a few minutes of prayer this gifted priest said: "I think you were nearly drowned when you were a small boy." Immediately the man recalled a forgotten memory. Yes, he had fallen from his father's shoulders into a shallow stream when he was three years of age. He had nearly drowned. The priest prayed that the strong fear involved in this traumatic memory would be healed. That was over ten years ago. The man has had no claustrophobia since. So prayer for inner healing can be very helpful.

3. *Focus on the Unconditional Mercy of God*
Since the shadow self can lead us into those sins that lower our self-esteem and weaken our relationship with God, it is important that we focus on the unconditional mercy of God.

One story that helps me to do this was told by St Thérèse of Lisieux. A rabbit was eating grass in a field. Suddenly it heard the distant sounds of a bugle blowing, dogs barking and horses galloping. It looked over its shoulder in fear. It could see a king together with his courtiers out on the hunt. Clearly, they had already picked up her scent and were heading in her direction, so the rabbit took off across the fields. Eventually she ran out of energy. Soon the dogs had surrounded her. They snarled with teeth bared. They were waiting for the king, who was already dismounting, to slay the rabbit. Then they would pounce. She looked up at the king. His hand was on his sword. He was about to draw it. The rabbit thought to herself: "If I don't do something quickly, I'm finished!"

She decided to use her remaining energy to jump up onto the king's outstretched arm. So she hopped up. With eyes full of desperation and pleading she looked into the eyes of the King. When his gaze met hers something melted in his heart. His swordgrip weakened. He began to stroke the rabbit with his other hand.

"I'm bringing this little creature back to the court", he said. "My children can play with it."

Thérèse said that in this parable the rabbit is the soul. The dogs are our sins that pursue us and threaten to devour us. The king is the Lord. The sword is his justice, which in justice he is entitled to use against us.

"But there is a fatal flaw in the heart of the king," says Thérèse. "If you look only into the eyes of his mercy, expecting only mercy, you will receive only mercy."

This profound intuition lies at the heart of the Gospel of God's mercy. As St. Paul wrote: "For those who are in Christ Jesus, there is now no condemnation." (Rm. 8:1). So when we as Christians who have been baptised into Christ, look into his eyes of endless mercy, we experience an inner cleansing from a sense of guilt. Self-esteem improves, our relationship with God is strengthened.

4. Forgive Those Who Have Hurt You

We have seen how low self-esteem can be traced back to a lack of unconditional love in childhood and to all kinds of hurts experienced down the years. As a result one of the principal way in which we can experience inner healing and therefore growth in self-esteem is to forgive those who have hurt us. In his book, *Sadhana: A Way to God* Anthony de Mello, S.J. suggests the following method:

"Imagine you see Jesus hanging on the Cross . . . Take all the time you need to picture him in vivid detail . . .

Now recall the reason for your resentment . . . Stay with it for a while . . .

Return to Jesus Crucified and gaze at him again . . .

Keep alternating between the event that caused your resentment and the scene of Jesus on the Cross . . . until you notice the resentment slipping away from you and feel the freedom and joy and light-heartedness that follows."

For more on this see Chapter One.

5. Focus on the Unconditional Love of God

We have seen above how people with low self-esteem tend to suffer from false images of God and associated negative feelings and attitudes. It can be liberating and healing to contemplate the unconditional love of God. The following exercise has helped me.

—Relax your mind and body as best you can.

—Affirm in faith that God is present.

—Recall the following words of scripture:

- "God is love" (1 Jn. 4:16)
- "As the Father loves me, so I love you" (Jn. 15:9)
- "I pray that you may have your roots and foundation in love, so that you, together with all God's people may have the power to understand how broad and long, how high and deep, is Christ's love. Yes, may you come to know his love—although it can never be fully known—and so be completely filled with the very nature of God" (Eph. 2:18).

—Imagine that Jesus is kneeling before you with a towel around his waist. Notice that he is looking at you with eyes filled with love and humility. He is not there to tell you what he wants. Rather he wants to know what you want from him (*Pause and let yourself respond*).

—Listen to Jesus as he says these words to your heart:

"I love and accept you just as you are. You don't have to change to receive my love. You don't have to improve, or to give up your sinful habits. Obviously I would want you to do so. But that is not a condition for receiving my love and acceptance. That you have already, before you change, even if you never decide to change. Do you believe me? Do you believe that I accept and love you as you are, shadow and all? Ponder what I'm saying to you and tell me how you feel."

I have found that an exercise like this can do wonders for my self-esteem. As I am grasped by the unconditional love of God a deep healing takes place in the depths of my personality.

Affirming Others

At the beginning of this section we noted Mother Teresa's view that many people in developed countries are victims of the famine of lovelessness. As a result they suffer from hurts and low self-esteem. They are in need of affirmation. The word in English comes from the Latin meaning "to make firm". It is very similar in meaning to the Greek word *Paraclete*, which is used to describe the Holy Spirit. It literally means "the Comforter, the one who gives strength". When we affirm a person we carry out a ministry on behalf of the Spirit, by "comforting others in their afflictions with the very comfort we ourselves received from God" (2 Cor. 1:4).

How do we go about affirming one another? Firstly by emphatic listening. Carl Rogers puts it this way. "Can I care while allowing the other to be separate? Can I leave the comfortable familiar structures of my own self to enter the unfamiliar territory of another, knowing I may never be the same, that from another viewpoint I could appear wholly deficient? Have I the strength not to be destroyed by his anger, frightened by his anguish, engulfed by his dependence, while accepting the integrity of both our points of view? Can I tread sensitively and intelligently on the precious mental "furniture" of another?" By listening in this way, we become God's answer to the cry of those who need comfort and affirmation. Secondly we can help people to grow in self-acceptance, by overlooking their weak points and drawing attention to their talents, gifts and achievements, no matter how small. As. St. Paul wrote: "In conclusion, my brothers, fill your minds with all those things that are good and that deserve praise: things that are true, noble, right, pure, lovely, and honourable . . . and the God who gives us peace will be with you" (Phil. 4:8-10).

3
Overcoming Stress

A Personal Experience of Stress

A few years ago I headed off with two colleagues to conduct a parish mission. Normally I would have been enthusiastic. But not on this occasion. Instead I dreaded the prospect of meeting strangers and dealing with their many problems.

On our very first morning in the parish I got off to a bad start. I became quite abrasive with a woman who had annoyed me. Afterwards I felt rotten. Why had I lost my self-control in such an unreasonable and hurtful way? I began to realise that I did not feel well. I was tense, up-tight and reluctant to face any kind of pressure. So I came to a difficult and embarrassing decision. It would be better for the team, the parishioners and myself if I withdrew from the mission.

For the next few months I felt miserable. I could not sleep well. I always felt tired. I got many dull headaches. They could last for days and were unaffected by aspirin. I felt anxious and apprehensive all the time. On one or two occasions I felt a real sense of panic. Over and over again, I asked myself the question, "What is happening to me?" I did not really know, but I was determined to find out.

Then as a result of a lot of reading and reflection, I came to recognise that I was suffering from "burn-out". It is a form of emotional exhaustion which is brought on by unhealthy levels of unrelieved stress. Some of it had been triggered by outer environmental factors such as the demanding nature of my work. Still more had been occasioned by inward psychological causes such as an exaggerated fear of failure.

But there was reason for hope . I began to realise that the pain of stress is nature's red light. It was warning me that the way I was living was not working. It was inviting me to make the necessary psychological and environmental changes that would help me to recover. Over a period of time I came to terms with these issues. I learned to relax and so regained my sense of personal well-being and peace.

Carl Jung once wrote: "There is no growth in consciousness without pain." Looking back, I can see how the experience of stress was for me a blessing in disguise. It forced me to take stock in many ways. As a result I grew in self-awareness and made a number of practical changes in my lifestyle. St. Paul says that we are comforted in our troubles "so that we may be able to comfort those who are in any trouble with the comfort with which we ourselves are comforted". (2 Cor. 1;4). Hence these pages are written in the belief that, if you or someone you care about suffers from unhealthy levels of stress, it can and should be overcome. Stress is an invitation to change and to grow.

The Nature of Stress

Stress is nervous tension. We have already noted that it can be caused by environmental and psychological factors. These can lead to either *acute* or *chronic* stress. Stress is acute when it is sharp but short-lived. By and large, it does not do us much harm. Indeed it may be helpful in the sense that it adds an extra edge to our performance, e.g. when running in a race or acting in a play. Stress becomes chronic when it persists in an unrelieved way. Combining these points we can look at a number of examples

1. *Acute environmental stress* could be experienced when a person has to move quickly to catch a valuable vase as it falls from the mantelpiece.

2. *Chronic environmental Stress* could be experienced by a person who has to work in an extremely noisy factory.

3. *Acute psychological stress* could occur as a result of hiccupping during an important speech.

4. *Chronic psychological stress* could be the outcome of having to cope with a bad marriage to an alcoholic partner.

So stress can be triggered by any number of things. But in the last analysis it is a largely subjective event. *It depends on the person's reaction—not on an outside event.* That said, the experience of stress is always the same. Nature has equipped us to cope with perceived dangers. In an emergency situation the body goes on alert. Automatically the brain triggers a sequence of physiological changes. Hormones in the form of adrenalin are produced. Digestion slows. Blood pressure rises. Perspiration increases. The eyeballs retract, while the pupils and also the nostrils and bronchi dilate. Sugars and fats are secreted to provide the body with extra energy. Muscles grow tense, ready for "flight or fight". This primitive reaction was very helpful when our ancestors had to cope with life and death situations. After all, they had to face regular attacks from either animals or enemies. It gave them the extra strength they needed to take appropriate action. As a result of their vigorous efforts their emergency supplies of energy were used up, and so they returned to a state of relaxation.

While the challenges and demands of modern life are many, they are rarely life-threatening. Even when they are, e.g. having to brake suddenly to avoid an accident, we do not really need the extra energy the body supplies. All we do is to move one foot to jam on the brakes. When the emergency has passed we remain keyed-up because we have not used up our bonus energy. The same is true when we are faced by the lesser crises of everyday life, such as deadlines to meet, appointments to keep, bills to be paid, etc. As a result our "flight or fight" response is activated over and over again in an inappropriate way. Stress levels go up so that acute stress becomes chronic. If it remains unrelieved it can have harmful physical, psychological and spiritual effects.

A Simple Stress Test

At the Gershom Centre in England, clients are given the following list of twenty signs of stress and asked to tick off the ones they are currently experiencing. Why not do the test yourself?

1. Rheumatic pains
2. Swollen glands
3. Breathlessness
4. Tingling sensations
5. Diarrhoea
6. Urinary and gynaecological problems
7. Stomach pains
8. Asthma
9. Mouth Ulcers
10. Depression
11. Dizziness
12. Palpitations
13. Blackouts
14. Insomnia
15. Headaches or migrane
16. Exhaustion
17. Allergies
18. Nausea
19. Tension
20. Skin rashes

If you are suffering from four or more of these symptoms for a period of a month or more you are probably suffering from unhealthy levels of stress.

Transitional Crises and Stress

While we can experience stress at any time in our lives, it is more likely to occur during times of painful change. Cardinal Newman once observed that "to live is to change". This is biologically true. Apparently every cell within us is replaced every seven years or so. We change psychologically and spiritually also. This is particularly true during times of personal crisis. These are *the* turning points for better or for worse in our lives.

There are two main types of crisis, predictable and unpredictable.

Psychologists say that *predictable crises* occur regularly throughout our lives. They precede the main developmental phases, e.g. before the onset of early, middle and late adulthood. Daniel Levinson says that these transitions occur between the ages of 17 and 22 , 40 and 45, and 60 and 65 approximately. He also indicates that we can expect lesser transitions between the ages of 28 and 33, and again between 50 and 55 approximately. The purpose of these crises is to urge us to tackle some specific developmental task. By doing so we grow into a new depth of maturity. *Unpredictable crises* occur when the "slings and arrows of outrageous fortune" come our way. We may be pitched into a period of turmoil and soul-searching by the death of a close relative, the news that we have cancer or by the loss of our job.Often a predictable crisis will occur at the same time as one or two unpredictable ones. Transitional crises of either kind have a three fold structure.

1. Onset of restlessness

A woman could face a predictable crisis with the onset of the menopause. At the same time she might have to cope with the fact that her husband has lost his job and that her unmarried daughter has become pregnant. Like countless other people she enters a time of painful transition. She may feel that she is losing control over her life. She lives in a sort of emotional "no man's land" where things happen to her. She feels like a victim. Troubling feelings seep up from the unconscious levels of her experience, e.g. anxiety, fear, insecurity, guilt, confusion, mild depression, etc. She enters a stressful period because her life seems subject to anonymous threats that evoke her "flight or fight" response on a daily if not an hourly basis.

2. Darkness and exploration

Times of crisis for a woman like this are often times of disillusionment. The way she looked at herself and her priorities is challenged. Beliefs and values that sustained her in the past seem strangely inadequate now. Not surprisingly, she loses her inner sense of joy and peace. Instead she feels agitated and restless. As the scaffolding that supported her self-image is removed, there can be a real sense of loss and grief. Her sense of hurt may give rise to a feeling of anger with herself, with others, and perhaps with God. Like many others she may try to repress these feelings. As a result they could turn inwards to attack her, thereby making her feel more insecure, inadequate and helpless. This kind of dynamic can lead to a lot of strain and tension.

During a crisis all kinds of questions surface:

• Why is my self-esteem so low?
• Why is it that I am always trying to please others and to win their approval?

• Why am I a perfectionist and so hard on myself when I fail?
• Why am I driven by a sense of obligation, rather than being motivated by personal conviction?
• Why am I always in a hurry with too many things to do?
• Why do I have so little time for friends or leisure activities?
• How come I cannot stand up for myself and assert my dignity and rights when I am being badly treated?
• When there is an argument or conflict of any kind, why do I need peace at any price?

These and many other questions can arise during a time of transition. They are important. They may be pointing to the largely unconscious attitudes and assumptions that have been causing so much stress in our lives.

Resolution and restabilisation

As our defence mechanisms begin to crumble during a time of crisis, we may get in touch with basic questions to do with our identity and values. As we answer them we begin to let go of our former assumptions and attitudes. As we do so, we embrace more appropriate and realistic ones. For example, the menopausal woman with family problems may discover that all her life she has been too preoccupied with public opinion. As she becomes more inner-directed her sense of security increases while her feelings of stress grow weaker.

The Signs and Effects of Unrelieved Stress

The Signs of Physical Stress

When a person is suffering from physical tension it can have the following knock-on effects on different parts of the body,

1. *Cardiovascular*: palpitations, racing heart, dizziness, faintness, fear of losing consciousness, blushing, migraine headaches, cold hands and feet.

2. *Respiratory*: unable to get enough air, hyperventilation i.e. fast, shallow breathing, chest constriction.

3. *Muscular*: tension headaches, shaking, severe weakness, restless body or legs, jaw grinding.

4. *Gastrointestinal*: butterflies in the stomach, nausea, vomiting, wind, flatulence, burping, abdominal pain, cramps and diarrhoea.

The Effects of Chronic Physical Stress

1. It can directly cause such problems as high blood-pressure. This in turn can lead to kidney disease, strokes and heart failure. All of these conditions can be life-threatening. Stress can also cause ulcers, asthmatic problems, build-up of cholesterol, etc.

2. It can aggravate conditions such as back-ache, arthritis, multiple sclerosis, allergies, skin conditions, hyperthroidism, etc.

3. It weakens the body's defence system. As a result it is more vulnerable to infections of all kinds, e.g. the common cold, flu and even cancer.

As we saw earlier, it is estimated by the medical profession that at least 60 per cent and possibly 80 per cent of all sickness is stress-related.

The Signs of Psychological Stress

There are many signs of psychological tension e.g. feeling anxious, social fears, fear of heights, or darkness, or being alone, low self-esteem, sleeping difficulties, etc.

The Effects of Chronic Psychological Stress

1. The person may suffer from panic attacks, a feeling of inner terror.

2. The person finds it hard to cope with any pressure. He suffers from outbursts of impatience, anger and hostility.

3. His concentration slips, he makes mistakes more often, e.g. locking the keys in the car . . . while the engine is running! Mental blocks are common, e.g. forgetting appointments and names. Sleep is disturbed by

many dreams and nightmares. Afterwards the person gets up feeling tired and tense.

4. The victim of stress may try to escape the pain of his condition in ways that reinforce the problem.

> • Eating has been called "nature's tranquilliser". If a stressful person eats too much he will feel guilty as his weight goes up. As a result his self-esteem will drop while his stress levels rise.
> • Many people suffering from stress feel thirsty and tired, so they drink endless cups of coffee and tea. Both tannin and caffeine are stimulants that increase stress.
> • Many people try to deaden the pain of stress with alcohol. It is true that it may relax a person for a time. It may make it easier to get off to sleep, but the sleep will be shallow as a result. And so the drinker will get up feeling tired and ill-equipped to meet the challenges of a new day. In some cases alcohol abuse can lead to addiction, accidents, domestic strife, loss of job etc.—all of which are stressful.
> • In an emergency situation tranquillisers and sleeping pills can be helpful, if they are prescribed for a short period, i.e. six weeks at the most. But if the stressful person comes to rely on them, they become part of the problem instead of being part of the solution.
> • It is commonly thought that smoking has a tranquillising effect. Perhaps the oral activity, reminiscent of being breast-fed, is reassuring, but nicotine is a stimulant and so increases stress. Many of the illnesses that come from smoking do not do much for stress levels either.

5. Chronic stress can lead to all kinds of physical problems, e.g. irregular periods in women and impotence in men. These difficulties reinforce stressful feelings.

6. Unrelieved stress can lead to "burn-out" or "compassion fatigue" as it has sometimes been called. Jerry Edelwich has described it as a "progressive loss of idealism, energy and purpose experienced by people

in the helping professions". That would include individuals such as social workers, counsellors, therapists, spiritual directors, doctors, nurses, chaplains and clergymen of all kinds. In my experience "burn-out" can afflict anyone, e.g. housewives, journalists, broadcasters, police men and women, dentists, pilots, etc. According to psychologists, "burn-out" has three degrees of severity.

The first degree of "burn-out" is common. Warning signs include an inability to shake off a lingering cold, frequent headaches and sleeplessness. That said, the person continues to work without much sign of trouble.

The second degree of "burn-out" occurs when the symptoms of the first stage consolidate and get worse. The person suffers from fatigue, prolonged headaches, angry outbursts, irritability and impatience. He worries too much about problems and may treat other people badly. For example, somebody who is normally polite and considerate ends up shouting at his colleagues. At this stage job-performance begins to suffer. The person becomes more detached and impersonal while saying "It's not that I don't want to help, I can't". Paradoxically, instead of taking things easier, typical sufferers take on extra work. But instead of achieving more, they actually accomplish less while reinforcing their stress.

The third degree of "burn-out" occurs when the symptoms become chronic. At this stage the person is unable to function normally. Physical sickness is common, e.g. heart-attacks, high blood-pressure, etc. Psychological difficulties are to be expected, e.g. severe depression, feelings of extreme loneliness and isolation, together with suicidal inclinations.

The Spiritual Effects of Chronic Stress

The experience of "burn-out" can be the outcome of a psycho-spiritual crisis in the personality. Let me explain why. St. Paul writes: "Do not model yourselves on the behaviour of the world around you, but let your behaviour change, moulded by your new mind." (Rom. 12:2). Plaster models are made in rubber moulds. As a result they assume the shape of the mould. Unconsciously, our sense of self and values can be moulded by the world rather than by the Lord and his values.

The secular self has a number of characteristics. Its sense of worth is secretly dependent on such things as success, reputation and status. It has a compulsive desire to acquire and defend these things, and a lurking fear of losing them. It tends to reject any experience from the outer or inner world that might threaten its sense of security and control.

During the kind of transitional crises we have already mentioned the things that have been supporting the secular self are removed. Instead of enjoying success, status and a good reputation, a person may have to drink the bitter wine of failure, loss and humiliation. The embattled victim will put up stiff resistance to this process. That can explain why he works frantically to retain the very things his secular self needs for a sense of well-being. As he loses the struggle, the sufferer is filled with fear, anger, hurt, etc. Often these feelings are repressed in a way that creates a lot of tension and strain. As this dynamic predominates, the secular self begins to run out of energy. It begins to suffer from a deep-seated exhaustion or "burn-out". The joy and peace of the past give way to spiritual desolation. Feelings of restlessness, agitation, hopelessness and sadness take hold.

The Lord seems distant and unreal. Prayer is often abandoned or becomes formal. The person goes through the motions, but his heart is no longer in it. Spiritual things hold little or no attraction, while the things of the world and the flesh seem very attractive. Temptation is strong and weakness common.

When it hits rock bottom, the personality can hit the "Rock of Ages". This happens in two stages. Firstly, the person feels a heartfelt desire for a new experience of God. Secondly, the Lord answers this desire by revealing his love. This can have the effect of refocusing the personality. It begins to move away from false, worldly values, to become more centred on Christ and his gospel. In this way St. Paul's advice is fulfilled: "You must give up your old way of life. You must put aside your old self, which gets corrupted by following illusory desires." (It is this old self that suffers from stress and "burn-out"). Your mind must be renewed by a spiritual revolution so that you can put on the new self that has been created in God's way." (Eph. 4:22-23) I should point out in passing that stress and desolation of spirit are not necessarily synonymous. Many people turn to the Lord with renewed energy during times of strain, seeking his help. In cases like this stress can be seen as a providential opportunity of developing an even deeper relationship with the Lord.

Overcoming Stress by Means of Relaxation Exercises

Perhaps the most helpful thing a stressful person can do is to use a relaxation exercise. There are many of them, e.g. yoga, reflexology, imagery training, etc. We will look at three examples that I have found helpful—Benson's Relaxation Response, Schultz's Autogenic Training and Sandford's Serenity Exercise.

The Relaxation Response

Dr. Herbert Benson was a professor of medicine at Harvard Medial School. His main interest was in high blood-pressure, which is often stress-related. He heard that experts in Transcendental Meditation had claimed that they could influence their autonomic functions such as heart rate and blood pressure. Benson thought that this was highly unlikely because the autonomic system is self governing and, by all accounts, beyond the influence of mind or will. However, he invited some of these experts in TM to participate in clinical trials which could put their claims to the test. In the event, he was surprised to find that they could indeed lower their blood-pressure without the use of drugs.

Benson analysed the TM technique. Having stripped it of its Hindu content, he found he could produce a secular version. It all depended on concentration. During times of stress the mind flits restlessly from one thing to another. It cannot focus on any single item for long. So TM tries to bring about tranquillity by encouraging meditation in a concentrated way on a meaningless word or *mantra*.

Benson wondered if it would not be better to use a word or phrase that would express the person's faith. He had a medical motive for this, based on the "placebo effect". Simply stated, it refers to bodily changes produced by beliefs and expectations. As Benson writes: "We know that any treatment is more likely to be successful if the patient has a great deal of faith in his physician's ability—or even faith that a higher spiritual power is at work in the body." As a Christian I believe that there is such a higher power at work within the human body; we call it the Holy Spirit. Further,

I am convinced that when a person receives the Spirit in baptism, he also receives the peace and harmony of God. As a result I am sure that this peace is within us as all times, even when we are experiencing stress. It is like a treasure buried in the field of the heart. Therefore I can say without hesitation: *"The peace I want is within"*. This phrase expresses my faith.

Benson says that the placebo effect is mobilised by using such a phrase as part of the secularised T.M. technique. Together they form the Relaxation Response, which can be outlined as follows:

1. Sit in a comfortable position.

2. Close you eyes, smile inwardly and relax your muscles.

3. Focus on your breathing. Breathe slowly and naturally.

4. Select a word or phase that expresses your faith conviction e.g. *"maranatha"* (which in Aramaic means "come Lord Jesus") or "the peace I want is within" (this is the ideal length for a mantra because it is seven syllables long). This word or phrase is repeated slowly on each outward breath. The key to the exercise is to try to think of nothing other than the words you are saying to yourself. In this connection Benson quotes the *Catholic Encyclopaedia* with approval: "Attention is the very essence of prayer; as soon as this attention ceases, prayer ceases."

5. When distracting thoughts intrude and upset your attention, disregard them gently by saying something like: "Oh well." Then quietly return to the word or phrase you are using. It is essential to maintain a passive relaxed attitude in dealing with any interruptions. Do not try to force yourself to attend. This will only make you tense and anxious about not succeeding.

If this exercise is followed for twenty minutes a day, two things will happen. First, you will get used to using it. Second, it will have a very calming effect.

Autogenic Training
Dr. Johannes Schultz pioneered autogenic training as a means of relaxation in the 1920's. Over the years it has been perfected by other researchers, notably Dr. Wolfgang Luthe. This method used verbal cues to influence

the autonomic system in order to produce deep relaxation. It is similar in many ways to the Relaxation Response in which one focuses attention on a word or phrase, while autogenic training focuses attention on physical sensations. So the key to this form of exercise is a sort of auto-suggestion called *"Passive Concentration"*, which affirms that the body is getting heavy and warm. I often use it.

First, I try to become aware of the sensations in my feet, noticing whether they are warm or cold, tense or relaxed. Then I imagine that they are getting heavy and warm. After a while I usually begin to sense the warmth. I focus my attention on that sensation and affirm that it is getting stronger. This is not done by a determined act of will. On the contrary it is a matter of believing that the gift of warmth is there to be discovered, so to speak. Having spent some time on my feet I might move to my hands and arms in a similar way. As I go through the exercise I can sense the tension leaving my muscles and a lovely feeling of relaxation spreading through my body. Here is a brief outline of the method.

1. Deep breathing exercises
    (a) Imagine ocean waves rolling in . . . and out.
    (b) Silently say to yourself: "My breathing is smooth and rhythmic."

2. Heartbeat regulation exercises
    (a) Imagine ocean waves.
    (b) Silently say: "My heartbeat is slow and regular."

3. Blood flow
    (a) Right arm and hand
    —Silently say: "My right arm and hand are heavy and warm."
    —Imagine the warm sun shining on them.
    (b) Left arm and hand
    —Silently say: "My left arm and hand are heavy and warm."
    —Imagine the warm sun shining on them.
    (c) Legs and feet
    —Silently say: "My legs and feet are heavy and warm."
    —Imagine the warmth flowing down from the arms and into the hands.

4. Summing up phrase
   "I am calm."

5. Return to activity
   Move again from step one to step three.

A Serenity Exercise

Mrs. Agnes Sanford was one of the pioneers in the rediscovery of the ministry of healing. In 1949 she published a book, *The Healing Light*, which has since become a classic. In it she describes a prayer exercise that I have adapted slightly.

1. Lay aside your cares and worries as best you can. Quieten your mind and concentrate on the reality of God. You may not know the Lord in a personal way. But you know that something sustains the universe. That something is not ourselves. So the first step is to remind yourself that there is a source of life outside yourself.

2. The second step is to get in touch with the source of life by saying a prayer like this: "Heavenly Father, please increase in me at this time your life-giving power." If you do not know this outside life as your heavenly Father, you could simply say: "Whoever you are—whatever you are—come into me now."

3. The third step is to *believe* and *affirm* that the power is coming into you. Recall what Jesus promised: "Whatever you ask for in prayer, believing you have it already, it will be yours." (Mk. 11:24). Accept the power in faith. No matter how much you ask for something, it only becomes yours as you *accept* it and give thanks for it. "Thank you," you can say, "that your life is *now* coming into me and increasing life in my body, mind and spirit."

4. The fourth step is to *observe* the operations of that life. In order to do this, you must decide on some tangible thing that you wish to be accomplished by that power, e.g. a decrease in stress and an increase of inner peace. You could say something like this: "I thank you Lord, that

the relaxation and peace I desire is being revealed within me, by the light of your Spirit."

As we come to the end of this section, a final recommendation. Nowadays you can buy relaxation tapes in many shops. As you play them on a tape recorder you follow the instructions of the speaker. A man who uses one, last thing at night, told me that he never heard the end of it, because he always fell asleep first. Listening to certain types of music can also be relaxing. There are many studies demonstrating the relaxing physiological responses to music, including changes in breathing, heart-rate, blood-rate, blood-pressure, blood supply, and galvanic skin responses. Some of the music of J.S. Bach is ideal for the purpose, e.g. his *Concerto for Two Violins*, his *Harpsichord Concerto in F Minor for Flute and Strings* and finally, his *Solo Harpsichord Concertos in F Major and C Major*. The bigger record stores also sell what is called "New Age Music", which is very relaxing.

Overcoming Stress by Means of Changes in Lifestyle

In 1943 Reinhold Niebuhr wrote the following prayer: "God give us the grace to accept with serenity the things that cannot be changed, courage to change the things which should be changed, and the wisdom to distinguish the one from the other." The experience of chronic stress is an invitation to change the aspects of our lifestyle that contribute to it. They can and should be changed.

Establish Priorities

It is important to discriminate between *needs* and *priorities*. Otherwise you will be swamped by an endless succession of urgent needs.

A few years ago I had a chat with Sean, a curate in a Dublin parish.

"What are your priorities from a personal point of view?" I asked.

"I must admit," he replied, "that I haven't given the thing much thought."

"As you think about it now," I said, "what would you like your top priority to be?"

Sean reflected for a while, then he said: "I think that parish visitation should be my number one priority."

"Well, do you get much time to visit?" I asked.

"Frankly, no," Sean replied, "other things seem to demand my attention. For example last night I had to attend a committee meeting. Tonight I'm judging a beauty competition in a local hotel. It's like that all the time."

"But if pastoral visitation is a priority", I retorted, "wouldn't it be better to say 'no' to the many invitations you receive. You would feel that you are doing something really worthwhile, instead of feeling guilty about not visiting."

The curate was no different from countless other people. Because he had failed to discriminate between needs and priorities he was hassled in a stressful way by countless demands on his time.

We begin to take control of our lives when we begin to establish long-term and short-term goals, i.e. for the following year and the following day. Having made a list of between five and ten long-term goals, try to number them in their order of importance, 1, 2, 3, etc.

Then try to work out a practical plan which indicates what has to be done and when. It is much the same when it comes to short-term goals for the following day.

I read an interesting story in this connection.

The president of an American steel company went to a New York consultant.

"I'll pay you any price," he said, " if you will tell me how to get more things done without undue stress."

The consultant replied: "At night spend five minutes analysing your problems of the following day.

"Write them down on a sheet of paper, but place them in their order of importance. Then tackle the first item as soon as you get to the office. Stick to it until it is finished. Then move to the number two and so on. Test this method as long as you like, and then send me what you think it is worth."

Some time later the consultant received a note from the company president. Enclosed was a cheque for $25,000 with the words, "For the most helpful advice I ever received."

Evidently the New York consultant knew about the Pareto Principle, or the 80/20 rule. It states that if a person has listed ten goals in their order of importance, and tackles the top two, eighty per cent of his potential effectiveness will be derived from them. Only twenty per cent of his effectiveness will be derived from the other eight! People who fail to discriminate between top priorities and lesser ones, can end up using a lot of energy achieving very little. So time management is really worthwhile. It increases efficiency, while protecting the person from the tyranny of having to respond to endless needs. In the name of worthwhile priorities we can say "no" with a good conscience. Instead of life controlling us, we can learn to regain control of our lives. As we do so, our stress levels will fall.

Exercise and Diet

When we looked at chronic stress we saw that feelings of distress are due to the fact that our bodies are reacting to excessive levels of adrenalin and other substances. What is needed is some way of reducing those levels. Our ancestors would have done this by means of vigorous "flight or fight".

We can have the same effect by taking exercise. It helps us to use up our surplus energy so that we feel more relaxed afterwards. Not only that, exercise helps us to become fit and contributes to our sense of well-being. There is also evidence to show that exercise enables the body to secrete chemicals that help to produce a state of physical harmony. Knowing this to be true, one American professor of psychology refuses to see stressful or depressed clients unless they are willing to take an hour's walk every day. So why not plan to take some form of regular exercise such as swimming, jogging, golf, etc. It is important that you enjoy the exercise and that you set realistic goals for yourself. Otherwise you will not keep it up. For example, walking is an excellent form of exercise. You could plan to take a half-hour walk five days a week. It needs to be energetic enough to stimulate the heart to greater efforts.

Besides taking exercise, diet too can help to control tension. First, it is important to avoid taking chemicals that increase stress, e.g. caffeine, tannin, salt, nicotine, sugar and the like. In many cases substitutes like decaffeinated coffee and artificial sugars can be used. Where this is not possible moderation is the key to success. If you are over-weight try to plan a sensible diet. In other words, do it slowly. As you lose surplus pounds in this way, you will feel better physically and emotionally. Your stress levels will go down, while your self-esteem will go up.

The Importance of Leisure

People suffering from stress often complain about all the work they *have* to do. Yet when they could take time off, they avoid doing so because they would be unable to relax and face themselves. As a result they tend to take on more work, thereby reinforcing their stress. The only way to break out of this vicious circle is to *decide* to take time off for recreation. This can be done in three ways, in personal reflection, sharing with friends, and pursuing hobbies.

It is refreshing to spend time with oneself, becoming aware of what is going on within. St. Augustine wrote in his *Confessions*: "Men go abroad to admire the heights and mountains, the mighty billows of the sea, the long courses of rivers, the vast extent of the ocean, the circular motion of the stars, and yet pass themselves by."

There is a story in the life of Dr. Carl Jung which illustrates the importance of this kind of self-intimacy. Apparently a society lady phoned him to request an urgent appointment at 3 p.m. the following Thursday. Jung said it would not be possible because he already had an important appointment at that very time. Well, on the Thursday the same lady happened to sail past Jung's garden which ran down to the shores of Lake Zurich. There was the famous doctor, his shoes off, sitting on a wall, his feet dangling in the water. As soon as she got home the irate woman rang Jung demanding an explanation.

"You told me," she exclaimed, "that you couldn't see me because you had an important appointment. Nevertheless I saw you at that very hour, whiling away the time at the bottom of your garden."

"I told you no lie," the doctor replied, "I had an appointment at that time, the most important of the week, an appointment with myself".

The purpose of time on one's own is fourfold. First, I listen to my own experience in order to *recover* my feelings which can often lurk unrecognised in the twilight zone of preconsciousness. Second, I try to *name* my feelings. Instead of saying "I feel good or bad about the invitation to the wedding", I try to be more specific about what I feel, e.g. "I feel delighted", or "surprised" or "scared" by the invitation. It is good also to see where those feelings are coming from. As John Powell once wrote: "Other people can stimulate my emotions, but the *causes* lie within." Our affective reactions are rooted in our past experiences, e.g. I am threatened and scared by the wedding invitation because I am not good at handling social occasions, especially when the people present are better educated and more sophisticated. I always feel stupid and inferior at times like that, just as I used to do when as a teenager I would ask a girl to dance. Third, I try to *own* my feelings, rather than thinking about them, or analysing them in a detached, dispassionate way. For example it would mean that instead of saying with a smile, "I seem to have a lot of anger within me" I would say with a frown, "I am very angry, because I feel hurt and humiliated." Fourth, it is good to *express* one's feeling, to a friend in conversation, and to God in prayer. Once I become aware of what is going on within me, and why, all sorts of issues can be faced and sorted out in a way that reduces stress.

Spending time with friends is also important. Our work requires us to fulfil all kinds of roles and to keep our thoughts and feelings to ourselves, especially when they are negative ones. It is great when we can share them with someone who is prepared to listen with empathy and understanding. We can let off steam with friends in the knowledge that they will accept and love us as we are, and not as we pretend to be. This kind of mutual communication can have a very soothing, therapeutic effect, especially for natural extroverts. Often they only discover what they are thinking and feeling as they talk. Otherwise they become frustrated, lonely and stressful. As Bacon once said: "The man or woman without friends becomes the cannibal of his own heart." For more on this point see the last chapter.

The pursuit of a hobby, such as music-making, painting, bird-watching, stamp-collecting, fishing, embroidery, woodwork, etc. can be relaxing and enjoyable. It is important to plan for leisure time. Unless this is a personal priority, it will be sacrificed in order to respond to all kinds of needs. The Comte de Mirabeau had the right idea when he wrote: "I would not exchange my leisure hours for all the wealth in the world." In my experience many people feel guilty about "wasting time" on hobbies. Perhaps this reaction is rooted in the unconscious assumption of the work ethic, that a person is only lovable for what he does and not for who he is.

Overcoming Stress by Changing Attitudes

Earlier it was stated that stress depends on a person's reactions, and not on outside events, e.g. having to talk in public could cause great stress in one person and none in another. The reason for the difference is psychological. Our reactions are rooted in our attitudes and beliefs, many of which can be unrealistic and unreasonable. In this section we are going to look at three such examples.

Irrational Beliefs

A well known psychologist called Ellis has suggested that our feelings about events are predetermined by our beliefs and perceptions. As a result he talks about the ABC of emotions. It can be outlined as follows:

A refers to the Activating event, e.g. being licked on the face by a big dog.

B refers to Beliefs about the events, for example:
- "The dog likes me"
- "Dogs can bite you for no apparent reason"
- "Dogs are lovely cuddly creatures"
- "Dogs are man's best friends, loyal and true"

Clearly, these kinds of beliefs are often rooted in a person's life experience. One person may have been bitten by a dog in childhood, while another may have happy memories of a family pet.

C refers to Consequent feelings, ones that follow from one's belief about the event. For example, the person who believes that dogs are unhygienic or liable to attack, is going to feel fear, while the person who thinks that they are cuddly and loyal, is going to feel attraction and love.

Ellis maintained that a lot of stressful negative feelings are due to the fact that our beliefs about reality are both unrealistic and unreasonable. He thought that stress could be reduced if and when such irrational beliefs were recognised and changed. He and his followers have listed many of the common ones. I will mention nine of them. See if any apply to you. Ask a friend what he or she thinks about your answers.

1. I need everyone's love and approval for about everything I do.
2. I should be able to do everything well.
3. If something bad could, or does happen, I should worry about it.
4. It is easier to avoid difficult tasks, than to try them and risk failure.

5. I will enjoy life if I avoid responsibilities and take what I get right now.
6. A person's worth is directly related to his objectively discernible productivity.
7. Anger is automatically bad and destructive, and should always be repressed.
8. People are very fragile and one should keep one's thoughts to oneself in order to avoid hurting others.
9. Happiness, pleasure, fulfilment and growth can only be achieved in the company of others, never on one's own.

Coping With Conflict in a Constructive Way

In relationships at home and at work, conflicts are inevitable. Here is a list of typical ones:

• Having to say "no" to a request for help.
• Coping with criticism from another person, e.g. the boss.
• Stating your rights and needs, e.g. in a restaurant.
• Expressing negative feelings such as anger.
• Giving a negative response to someone, having to confront them, e.g. telling a son or daughter they have to be home at midnight, not three in the morning.
• Differing from the majority opinion at a meeting.
• Making a request, e.g. asking a friend for money.
• Initiating social contacts, e.g. at a wedding where you know none of the guests.

There are two stressful and inappropriate ways of coping with conflict. The first, is to be *passive*, to back down because of lack of self-esteem and the consequent belief that one should work for peace at any price. For example, one has arranged to meet a friend at 3 p.m. at the GPO in Dublin. She does not turn up until 3.30 and offers no explanation. You feel hurt and angry, but you smile and say nothing. To bury anger like this causes frustration and stress.

The second way of coping with a conflict situation is to become *aggressive* and overbearing. So when the friend turns up late, you attack her verbally: "You are completely unreliable, your word means nothing. You don't give a damn about anybody." Granted this is a way of letting off emotional steam. But it is hurtful and will cause a rift between the two people and may evoke a counter-attack perhaps. Either way it will increase stress.

The third way of coping is to act *assertively*. When the friend arrives late I express what I feel: "I felt hurt and angry when you didn't turn up at the time we arranged. I felt let-down and taken for granted." In this way one lets off steam, but without attacking the other person and so stress levels can be reduced.

This assertiveness can be used in all kinds of situations. For example, you are making a point at a meeting, when someone rudely interrupts. You can respond in a positive way by saying: "Could you wait a moment, I want to finish my point, it is important to me."

The same approach can be used in a shop where you were sold a defective article. "The clock you sold me doesn't work correctly. I want a replacement." If the assistant begins to argue the point, do not get involved, keep on asserting your position: "The clock doesn't work. I want a new one please!" Many people find it hard to be assertive because of a lack of self-acceptance.

From Obligation to Personal Conviction

Many people suffer from what has been called "hardening of the oughteries". They are normally motivated by a sense of cheerless obligation, the "oughts, musts, and have-tos" of other people. As a result, they begin to lose touch with their own deeper desires and inner freedom. Consequently, they may feel that they are losing control of their lives, and are hapless pawns on the chessboard of life. They spend their lives trying to please other people, not out of love, but because of fear, and a fear of condemnation or criticism. Needless to say, this is a stressful experience.

The way to overcome this sense of suffocation is to get used to asking the question, "In the light of my beliefs, and values, what do I *want* in these circumstances?" On getting in touch with what is going on within, you will be in contact with your deepest self and your own freedom. As a result you will have an increased sense of autonomy and self-determination. You may do many of the same things as before, but for a different motive now.

Biblical Faith and Stress

The pace and pressures of modern life can be hectic. Crises of all kinds are common. If we learn to cope in the light of God's providence, we will cope much better. It is simply a matter of *nestling* in the Lord, rather than *wrestling* alone with difficulties. This point of view is illustrated over and over again in the Scriptures. We will examine one example from Chronicles 20 in some detail.

Facing Impossible Odds

The Jewish King Jehoshaphat received news that his kingdom was about to be attacked by a huge army. From a military point of view the position was hopeless. Not surprisingly, the king was filled with fear and disquiet. But instead of magnifying the problem by focusing his attention on it, he magnified the Lord by focusing on him by means of prayer and fasting.

Hearing God's Word and Comfort

Having poured out his heart to the Lord, Jehoshaphat waited for his response. It came through one of his priests. Inspired by the Spirit he said: "Your majesty, and all you people of Judah and Jerusalem, the Lord says you must not be discouraged or afraid to face this large army. *The battle depends on God and not on you.*" This prophetic word finds an echo many times in the Scriptures.

• In (Exodus 14:14)Moses says: "Do not be afraid. Stand firm and you will see the deliverance the Lord will bring you today. *The Lord will fight for you, you need only be still.*"

• Normally we translate (Psalm 37:7) as "Be still and know that I am God". However, it could be more accurately translated as "*Stop fighting, and know that I am God, supreme among the nations.*"

In other words, when faced with difficulties, trust the Lord, do what he says and see what he will do on your behalf.

Anticipating Victory in Praise

Knowing that God would be true to his word, King Jehoshaphat worshipped the Lord while his priests praised him with loud voices. The following morning the king "appointed men to sing to the Lord and to praise him for the splendour of his holiness as they went out at the head of the army". This is a typical example of what is known in Hebrew as the *teruwah Yahweh* or "victory shout". It was a religious war cry meant to strike terror into enemies and to anticipate the manifestation of God's saving help. For example the "victory shout" preceded the fall of Jericho. Again on Palm Sunday it anticipated the resurrection of Jesus and his victory over sin, Satan and death. The king and his people believed in the Lord, and as a result they came to see the victory that they had desired, and which God had promised. Their enemies were defeated. The Jews did not have to strike a blow.

The Way of Expressing Faith in Times of Stress

Having reflected on the biblical pattern of faith, we can go on to apply it in our own lives. There are three steps which spell the word THE.

- T refers to Thanking God no matter what happens.
- H refers to Handing your difficulties to the Lord.
- E refers to Expecting the Lord to help you.

Let us look at each step in turn.

Thanking God in All Circumstances
On a number of occasions in the New Testament we are told:

- "Pray constantly and for *all things* give thanks to the Lord" (1Thess. 5:18).
- "*Always* give thanks for *everything*, to God the Father" (Eph. 5:19).
- "If there is anything you need, pray for it asking God for it with prayer and *thanksgiving*" (Phil. 4:6-7)

No matter what pressures and demands we have to face, we should pray with praise and thanksgiving. We do so in the belief that God will bring good out of the negative circumstances of our lives. The notion of the "happy fault" lies behind this confidence in God's providence. It comes from the Easter liturgy, where the sin of Adam and Eve is referred to as a "happy fault . . . which gained for us so great a Redeemer!" St Paul echoed this insight when he wrote that by turning *everything* to their good, God co-operates with those who love him. (Rom. 8:28) Having poured out one's feelings of distress to the Lord, one goes on to express one's faith conviction to him in the form of praise and thanksgiving. In doing so, many of us have found that it opens the heart to the graces God wants to give.

Handing Our Difficulties to the Lord

In (1 Peter 5:7) we read: "Cast your anxieties on the Lord, for he cares about you." Anxieties seem to have a gravitational pull that draws our attention away from God to ourselves. As a result many of us seem to cling to our worries and cares. It takes an act of will to reverse this dynamic. We have to make a conscious decision to hand over our lives and our problems into the care of God as we understand Him.

Expect the Lord to Help You

When we trust the Lord we can be sure that he will comfort us. As St Paul says: "God helps us in all our troubles." (2 Cor. 1:4-5) No matter how weak and vulnerable we may feel, "God's power is made perfect in our weakness." (2 Cor. 12:8).

I had a memorable experience of this truth a couple of years ago. I had been invited to speak at a conference, for Italians only, in Assisi. When I got to Rome, en route to my destination, I was suffering from chronic stress. I was anxious about everything. What would I say at the conference? Would my interpreter be able to cope? Would I be able to find out what buses and trains I would need to get to my engagement? The more I thought about these things, the more my stress increased. I had a blinding headache. My body was like a wound-up spring. Finally, I turned to the Lord. I poured out my feelings, all of them negative. Having tried to thank the Lord, I implored him to help me. After a while I recalled a text in (Isaiah 41:10) "Fear not, I am with you, be not dismayed, for I am your God, I will strengthen you, I will uphold you with my victorious right hand."

"I will strengthen and uphold you." That was just what I needed to hear. I asked the Lord to carry out his promises. Nothing seemed to happen. I felt very disappointed, and told the Lord so. Then I went back to the verse and noticed that the Lord had said: "Fear not, be not dismayed." Perhaps this was not a word of advice, but rather a command. So I said to the Lord: "Be it done unto me according to thy word. If you want me to be courageous I *will* be courageous. I'll take on the whole of Italy if necessary. But you must help me."

Well, it was like a miracle. As soon as I said this prayer, a cloud of peace came upon me. My headache disappeared. My tension melted. Stress was replaced by a quiet confidence in the Lord. It never deserted me. I sailed through the conference without a worry. The Lord had been as good as his word.

Accept Divine Peace

Over a period of time I have come to appreciate the fact that there is a difference between physical relaxation and spiritual peace. Needless to say there is a connection between the two. But it is quite possible to imagine that a person would be suffering from stress while being at peace deep down in his heart, on account of having a good conscience and confidence in God's loving mercy. It is also possible to imagine that a person could be physically relaxed while being spiritually agitated and desolate for one reason or another.

During a recent visit to Medjugorje I was impressed by the messages that seem to come from Our Lady, Queen of Peace. I want to quote two of them. The first is for our everyday lives: "If you want to be very happy, live a simple, humble life, pray a lot, and don't worry and fret over your problems—let them be settled by God." The second message concerns the future: "Don't think about wars, chastisements, evil. It is when you concentrate on these things that you are on the way to enter into them. Your responsibility is to accept divine peace, live it."

Scripture Texts for Times of Stress

The following scripture texts may provide you with guidance and strength in times of stress:

1. *Joshua 1:9*
"Remember that I have commanded you to be determined and confident!

Don't be afraid or discouraged, for I, the Lord you God, am with you wherever you go."

2. *Isaiah 41:10*
"Fear not, for I am with you, be not dismayed, for I am your God; I will uphold you with my victorious right hand."

3. *2 Chronicles 20:15*
"The Lord says that you must not be discouraged or be afraid . . . the battle depends on God, not on you."

4. *Exodus 14:13*
"Do not be afraid! Stand by and see the salvation of the Lord which he will accomplish for you today . . . The Lord will fight for you while you keep silent."

5. *Jeremiah 17:7-9*
"But I will bless the person who puts his trust in me. He is like a tree growing near a stream and sending out roots to the water. It is not afraid when hot weather comes, because its leaves stay green; it has no worries when there is no rain; it keeps on bearing fruit."

6. *2 Chronicles 14:11*
"Yahweh, no one but you can stand up for the powerless against the powerful. Come to our help. Yahweh our God! We rely on you, and confront this crisis in your name. Yahweh, you are our God. Let man leave everything to you."

7. *Daniel 10:17-20*
"For now I have no strength, and no breath is left in me. Again one having the appearance of a man touched me and strengthened me. And he said: "Oh, man greatly beloved, fear not, peace be with you; be strong and of good courage."

8. *John 16:13*
"You will have peace by being united to me. The world will make you suffer. But be brave! I have overcome the world."

9. *Romans 8:31*
"If God is for us, who is against us?"

10. *Hebrews 13:5-7*
"The Lord has said: I will never fail you nor forsake you. Hence we confidently say: 'The Lord is my helper, I will not be afraid; what can man do to me'?"

11. *1 Peter 5:7*
"Cast all your anxieties on the Lord because he cares about you."

12. *Psalm 34:18*
"The Lord is near the brokenhearted, and saves the crushed in spirit."

13. *Mathew 11:29-30*
"Come to me, all who labour and are heavily laden, and I will give you rest. Take my yoke upon you, and learn from me, for I am gentle and humble of heart, and you will find rest for your souls."

> Prayer of St. Teresa of Avila
> *Let nothing perturb you,*
> *Nothing frighten you.*
> *All things pass.*
> *God does not change.*
> *Patience achieves everything.*
> *Whoever has God, lacks nothing.*
> *God alone suffices.*

4
Dreams—A Christian Understanding

The Science of Dreams

Divide your age by three. *That's* the amount of time you have spent sleeping. Now divide that number by five. That, surprisingly, is the amount of time you have spent dreaming! For example, a sixty-year-old man will have spent about twenty years sleeping and four years dreaming. He might be sceptical about these figures, protesting that he can only recall a few dreams. Research, however, has shown that while we forget about 90 per cent of our dreams, they punctuate our sleep every 90 minutes or so. Scientists in Chicago discovered this in the 50's. They noticed that dreaming is associated with rapid eye movements, called REM for short. If they woke up a volunteer during REM he or she would invariably be able to recall a dream. If they continued to disrupt the dreaming process of volunteers, their mental health suffered. Dreams then, seem to play an important role in the self-healing powers of the human mind.

At the beginning of this century Sigmund Freud and Carl Jung laid the foundations of modern psychiatry. Among other things, they studied the origin and meaning of dreams. They agreed that when the conscious mind is off-guard during sleep, dreams emanate from the cavernous depths of the unconscious self. "The dream", said Freud, "is the royal road to the unconscious." Jung described it as the theatre of the mind, "where the dreamer is at once scene, actor, prompter, stage manager, author, audience and critic".

Freud and Jung differed however when it came to the interpretation of dreams. Freud believed that these night-time videos of the mind were either explicit or symbolic representations of suppressed erotic desires. He wrote: "The more one is concerned with the solution of dreams the more one is driven to recognise that the majority of the dreams of adults deal with sexual material and give expression to erotic wishes." For example, a man might recall a dream in which he entered a church to pray, having opened the door with a large golden key. A Freudian interpretation would suggest that while the dream appears at first sight to be religious, it is really a disguised desire for sexual intercourse. The golden key is a symbol of the male sexual organ. The keyhole is a symbol of the female genitalia.

Jung's approach was different. While he accepted that some dreams were erotic in nature, many others gave expression to spiritual desires for wholeness and meaning. Unlike Freud, who thought that religious desires were a form of neurosis, Jung thought that neurosis was probable without them. In his book, *Modern Man in Search of his Soul*, he wrote: "In 30 years I have treated many patients in the second half of life" (i.e. over 35 years of age!) "Every one of them fell ill because he or she had lost that which the living religions in every age have given their followers, and none of them was fully healed who did not regain his religious outlook." So, like Freud, Jung believed that dreams were letters from the unconscious. Unlike Freud, however, he was of the opinion that some of them were written by the Spirit, on paper supplied by the psyche. If these letters, in particular, were opened and understood, they could become a source of divine revelation and healing. Recall, for example, the dream about entering the church in order to pray. It could be interpreted in a Jungian way by suggesting that the "key" to the man's desire for wholeness can be found in a deeper spiritual life, as symbolised by his entry into the church.

Dreams in the Ancient World

There was great interest in dreams in all ancient cultures. Aristotle, the famous Greek philosopher, was of the opinion that such pre-rational forms of religious experience were of no real importance because God was known by reason alone. Centuries later, Cicero the Roman author, was also critical of dreams. In his book, *Divination*, he maintained that the methods of interpretation current in his day were fanciful and useless. By and large he was probably correct.

In the second century A.D. the first scientific description of dreams was published. It was written by a Greek from Ephesus, named Artemidorus. His classic work, *Oneirocritica*, maintained that there were two basic kinds of dream. Firstly, there was the type that related to a person's present physical or mental state. A hungry man, for example, would dream of food. Secondly, there were dreams which had to do with the future. Because their messages were disguised in symbolism, they needed careful interpretation. Artemidorous outlined sensitive and subtle suggestions on this subject which have continued to have influence right down to our own day.

Dreams in the Old Testament

The Bible refers to dreams as "the dark speech of the Spirit". Like men and women of all ancient cultures, the Jews saw the dream as a way of getting in touch with the supernatural realm. Job wrote: "God speaks again and again, in dreams, in visions of the night when sleep falls on men as they lie on their beds. He opens their ears at times like that, and gives wisdom and instruction." (33:14). This point finds an echo in the Book of Numbers: "When there are prophets among you, I reveal myself to them in visions and speak to them in dreams." (12:6). In the Book of Sirach a more cautionary note is struck. "Dreams are nonsense," we read. "They are like the fantasies of a pregnant woman; unless sent as emissaries from the most high, do not give them a thought, for dreams have led many astray, and those that relied on them have come to grief."

On balance, the scriptural attitude is positive as far as dreams are concerned. This is obvious in the account of Joseph the dreamer and Daniel the prophet. Both men experienced the revelations of God in dreams. They were also gifted and inspired interpreters of dreams for the Egyptian Pharaoh and King Nebuchadnezzar.

Older Catholics may remember how the catechism maintained that dream interpretation was sinful. The reason for this curious point of view can be traced back to St. Jerome's translation of the Old Testament into Latin. The Hebrew word *qasam* refers to witchcraft and divination. Needless to say, the bible was against both (cf. Lev. 19:26 and Deut. 18:10). However, on a number of occasions St. Jerome translated the word *qasam* as dream interpretation, so that it shared in the condemnation of witchcraft. Until recently, the Church's position was based on St. Jerome's mistaken translation. It was ironic, because the saint's decision to devote his life to bible study was based on a revelation he received in a religious dream. A voice said to him: "You are a follower of Cicero, not of Christ." Jerome replied in the dream: "Lord, if ever again I possess worldly books, or if ever again I read such, I have denied you!"

Dreams in the New Testament

Dreams played an important role in the New Testament. The Gospel of Matthew tells us that Joseph received messages from God in his dreams on no less than four occasions. They concerned his marriage to Mary (1:20), the exile of the holy family in Egypt (2:13), their return (2:19) and their decision to settle in Galilee (2:22). On each occasion the revelation Joseph received enabled him to protect the child Jesus.

Later in Matthew's gospel there is a poignant account of yet another prophetic dream. During the trial of Jesus, Pilate's wife warned her husband in these words: "Have nothing to do with that innocent man, because in a dream last night I suffered much on account of him." (27:19) It was as if God the Father were trying to shield his beloved Son from injustice and pain. Tragically, Pilate knew nothing of the sensitivity and obedience of either Joseph or the wise men who had avoided Herod as a result of a dream. (Mt. 2:12)

In the Acts of the Apostles, we again find dreams linked with prophetic messages. On Pentecost morning St. Peter quoted the words of the prophet Joel: "I will pour out my Spirit on all flesh, and your sons and daughters shall prophesy, and your young men shall see visions, and your old men shall dream dreams." (3:1)

In the Bible in general it would seem that dreams and visions are closely related. A vision is a vivid and spontaneous type of daydream, inspired by God, when a person is awake. We find many examples of these dream-like visions in the lives of the apostles. St. Peter was prompted to take the momentous step of preaching the gospel to the gentiles as a result of a vision. (10:11 ff.) St. Paul was led to take a similar initiative when he came to preach in Europe as a result of a night time dream. (16:6-11) How different Christianity might have been if Peter hadn't preached to Cornelius, or Paul hadn't travelled to Greece.

Dreams in Christian Tradition

Tertullian expressed a common view of the early Church when he wrote: "Is it not known to all people that the dream is the most usual way that God reveals himself to man?" Perhaps Tertullian exaggerated a bit when he said that dreams were "the most usual" form of revelation. But they were certainly a common way of receiving inspiration. We will look at some of the many examples that are available from that period.

St. Augustine tells us in his *Confessions* that his mother, St. Monica, experienced many revelatory dreams and visions, mostly to do with his spiritual destiny. He says that Monica placed great reliance on them, and that she could discern the difference between natural and inspired dreams. "She always said that by some sense, which she could not describe in words, she was able to distinguish between your revelations and her own natural dreams." Monica's dreams came true when Augustine was converted to Christianity.

The Emperor Constantine converted to Christianity as a result of a dream in which Christ appeared to him bearing the first two letters of his holy name in Greek. The Lord told Constantine to have these two letters emblazoned on the flags and shields of his army before the decisive battle of the Milvian Bridge in 312 A.D. When victory was won, Christianity replaced paganism as the official religion of the Roman Empire.

It could be argued that two dreams played an important role in the conversion of the Irish to Christianity. In his *Confessions*, St. Patrick tells us, firstly, how he escaped from captivity: "In my sleep one night I heard a voice saying to me: 'It is well that you fast, soon you will go to your own country.' After a short while I again heard a voice saying: 'Look, your ship is ready.' It was quite a distance away, about 200 miles; I had never been to the place, nor did I know anyone there. I ran away and left the man with whom I had spent six years. The power of God directed my way successfully and nothing daunted me until I reached the ship." When

Patrick reached mainland Europe he was eventually ordained a priest. Then, when he was on a visit to his relatives in Britain, he had a second dream: "It was there one night I saw the image of a man called Victor, who appeared to have come from Ireland with an unlimited number of letters. He gave me one of them and I read the opening words which were: 'The voice of the Irish.' As I read the beginning of the letter I seemed at that same moment to hear the voice of those who were by the wood of Vocult, which is near the western sea. They shouted with one voice: 'Young man, we ask you to come and walk once more among us.' I was cut to the very heart and could read no more, and so I woke up. Thank God, after many years the Lord answered their cry." Patrick died around the year 480 A.D. In every century since then we find that saintly Christians have experienced the inspiration of God in their dreams, much as the Apostle to the Irish did. We will look at a few modern examples.

John Newton was converted in 1748 as a result of a religious experience. He had been a slave trader. During a visit to Derry city he had a religious dream, followed by a spiritual awakening in a city church. As a result he gave his life to Christ, became a minister, and worked the rest of his days for the abolition of slavery in the British Empire. He celebrated the mercy and goodness of God in his life in the well known hymn, *Amazing Grace.*

The miraculous medal was revealed by the Blessed Virgin to St. Catherine Labouré during a series of visions in 1830. Catherine had many religious dreams. She had joined the French Sisters of Charity as a result of one. It was about an old man she couldn't recognise. Some time later, when she was thinking of becoming a nun, she saw a picture of the old man displayed in a convent of the Daughters of Charity. It was Vincent de Paul. As a result Catherine joined the community he had helped to found with St. Louise de Marillac.

One of the most beautiful dreams I have come across was one recounted by St. Thérèse in a letter she wrote in 1896. She was ill at the time and going through a bout of desolation of spirit. Then one night she had a dream of saintly members of her order who had died. One of them, Venerable Anne of Jesus, who had founded the Carmilites in France, showed great affection and love for Thérèse. When she awoke she was filled with consolation. "I cannot express the joy of my soul since these things are experienced but cannot be put into words. Several months have passed since this sweet dream, and yet the memory it has left in my soul has lost nothing of its freshness and heavenly charms."

The Church's Changing Attitude to Dreams

It would seem that the Church has gone through at least three phases as far as dreams are concerned.

The first phase from the gospels up to the sixth century was one in which the Church welcomed religious dreams in the belief that they could be a means of revelation.

The second phase from the sixth to the 20th century was one in which religious dreams were regarded with suspicion. The change of attitude was noticeable in the teaching of Pope St.Gregory the Great (540-604 A.D.). While accepting the possibility of religious dreams, he thought it would take a saint to discern whether they were inspired by God or not. As a result, he urged the faithful to focus their attention on revealed truth as taught by the Church, rather than expecting private revelation in dreams. St. Thomas Aquinas reinforced this point of view in the 13th century. He was deeply influenced by the recently discovered writings of Aristotle. He shared this philosopher's view that God was known by the rational mind. Thomas was sceptical about the importance of pre-rational forms of religious experience such as speaking in tongues, prophecy, or religiously-inspired dreams. So perhaps it's not surprising to find that there is hardly a reference to the religious significance of dreams in the 11,000 pages of his massive *Summa Theologica*. As the theology of St. Thomas was adopted by the Catholic Church, the prejudice against dreams became official. That said, Christians continued to experience revelation in this attractive form, as we have seen.

The third phase began with the Second Vatican Council. It was one of rediscovery and openness. When the Council Fathers were discussing the *Document on the Church*, they wondered if they should include a paragraph on the gifts of the Spirit mentioned by St. Paul. (1 Cor. 12). The Pauline list mentions nine charisms. It includes such pre-rational forms of religious experience as miracles, the faith to move mountains, and discernment of spirits. When it came to the vote, the bishops decided to include a positive, open attitude to the charisms in paragraph twelve of the *Document on the Church*. They wrote: "Charismatic gifts, whether they be the most outstanding or the more simple and widely diffused, are to be received with understanding and consolation." Surely, religious dreams can be counted among those gifts that are "simple and widely diffused"!

How Revelation is Possible in Dreams

The Bible sees the human person as an inseparable unity of body, mind and spirit. St. Paul adverts to this when he prays: "May God . . . keep your whole being, spirit, mind and body, free from all fault." (1 Thess. 5:22).

What is the difference between the spirit and the mind? The *human mind* includes all our conscious and unconscious experiences such as thinking, feeling, memory and will. The *human spirit* is that part of a person which can only be satisfied by relationship with God. When we sleep we can have either a natural or a religious dream. The natural kind seems to have its origins in the mind alone. A religious dream has its origin in our human spirit. This is so because the Lord can reveal himself to our spirits by the action of the Holy Spirit, the Dreamer within. The Holy One dreams the dream by using our memories, feelings, and imaginations to express the revelation. Thus, a natural dream is a letter from the unconscious. A religious dream is a letter written by God himself in the chamber of the soul upon paper supplied by the psyche.

Four Kinds of Religious Dream

After a good deal of reflection. I have come to the conclusion that there are at least four kinds of religious dream.

- Firstly, there is the dream as religious solution.
- Secondly, there is the dream as spiritual counsellor.
- Thirdly, there is the dream as preparation for death.
- Fourthly, there is the dream as comforter and healer.

1. The Dream as Religious Solution

We bring our worries to bed. I can recall one such occasion when my prayers for God's help were answered with a memorable dream. I had been reluctant to pray for people because I had an exaggerated sense of my own unworthiness. I dreamt I was standing in the sanctuary of a small church with bare stone walls. Suddenly, the door opened, and in leapt St. Francis of Assisi and some of his companions. My eyes were riveted on the saint. To me he was the very epitome of holiness. Out of the corner of my eye I noticed a crippled boy. Francis moved toward him and gestured for me to join him. Then he asked me to put my hands on the boy's knees and to pray with him for healing. I was overjoyed when I could feel diseased bones moving back into their proper place. I glanced upward. Francis was gone. Joy turned into dismay. How could the healing be completed without him? Then I woke up.

As I reflected on the possible meaning of the dream I began to see what God was showing me. I had believed that God would only answer the prayers of very holy people and not those of a sinner like myself. Later that morning I happened to be reading the letter to the Philippians. I came to the verse: "For it is God who is at work *in you*, both to will and to work for his good pleasure." (Phil. 2:13). It was a flash of revelation, the answer to my dream. God is at work in *me*, in spite of my faults. As Paul wrote: "There is no condemnation now for those who live in union with Christ Jesus." (Rm. 8:1). From then on I had much more confidence in praying for people.

2. The Dream as Spiritual Counsellor

God can help us to get in touch with the urgings of the Spirit, with the holy desires he has planted within our hearts, by means of a dream.

A few years ago I was talking with a woman who was seriously ill. She told me that she had been raised as a Catholic but had stopped practising that faith some 30 years before. Then she told me about a dream she had experienced a few nights previously. It struck me as being religious in nature. I asked the woman what she made of her dream. She said that it seemed to uncover a deep longing within her to return home to the Church, so to speak, not as a matter of fearful obligation but as an expression of loving conviction. Shortly after that I had the joy of reconciling her to the Church when she received the sacraments.

3. The Dream as Preparation for Death

Research indicates that people with terminal illnesses tend to pass through different stages such as denial, bargaining, anger, depression, and finally acceptance. Dreams can help a person to accept death in a peaceful way.

I remember the case of a famous soccer player dying of cancer. He spoke about a dream that had influenced him deeply. In the dream he had just won a cup final and was going up to receive the trophy. When it was in his hands he noticed it was full of wine. He thought that he could hear a voice saying: "Will you drink from this chalice?" At first he felt inclined to do so, but then he thought: "This is the chalice of suffering. I won't drink from it." But the voice said a second time: "Will you not drink from the chalice I offer you?" He paused and replied, " For you Lord, I will drink."

When the dying man woke up he was filled with a sense of peace and acceptance which everyone noticed. Shortly afterwards he died a saintly death.

4. The Dream as Comforter and Healer

Dreams can be a source of comfort and healing in times of stress and grief, such as occurs after the death of a loved one.

A widow told me recently of the death of her beloved husband. She was distraught after the funeral and plagued with guilt feelings. Then one night she dreamt she was going up the stairs in her home. She opened a door and stepped into a room radiant with light. Her husband was there, standing in front of her, robed in a garment of glowing white. The woman walked toward him until he put his arms around her waist and embraced her. When she woke up this woman felt a profound sense of peace and contentment in knowing that her husband was in heaven. From that day forward her emotions began to heal and she was able to face life again with some enthusiasm.

Interpreting Dreams—Some Suggestions

1. Befriend Your Unconscious and Pray for Revelation

Like many others, I have found that I'm more likely to remember my dreams when I befriend my unconscious. Sometimes when I'm trying to deal with a confusing situation in everyday life, I say something like this: "Dear unconscious, I trust you. You know what's really going on. I need your help. I'd welcome a dream that would enable me to make sense of what I really feel." Believing that the Holy Spirit is the great Dreamer within, sometimes I put the request in the following way: "Dear Lord, the psalmist assures us that you bless those who love you even while they sleep. Please grant me a dream tonight which will help me to get in touch with reality as you see it. Amen."

2. Remember and Record Your Dreams

Researchers in the U.S. Navy dream laboratory at San Diego found that if a dream is not remembered within five minutes of waking, there is a 95 per cent chance it will be forgotten. As a result, it can be helpful to do the following things.

• Have a note pad beside your bed.
• Put the date on the top.
• Note your dreams as soon as you can in as much detail as possible

I have found that I haven't the discipline to record all my dreams, but I do try to write down the more significant ones, especially if they seem to be religious. For example, I jotted down the following dream on 18 July, 1986.

> I could see a youngish woman. Immediately I thought: "That's St. Thérèse of Lisieux." She wasn't wearing a Carmelite habit. She seemed to be clothed in a very simple dress made of wool. It was modest, reminiscent of the kind worn by peasants in movies. She had black hair. It was short, as if it were in a bun at the back. Her eyebrows were black, arched and striking. Her face was oval and sallow. She walked toward me and held out her arms to embrace me and give me a hug. I was surprised by this. I thought to myself: "I didn't think a saint would be as demonstrative as this!" At the same time it occurred to me: "This is a woman of love, she has to express her affection and tenderness." As Thérèse hugged me, I got a felling of unworthiness. I thought: "She won't be pleased by my shortcomings. No doubt she will warn me, and tell me I need to repent!" As I looked into Thérèse's face, I didn't sense any rejection, but I felt she was saying with her look: "You are right, your shortcomings must be tackled." I began to cry in an agitated way. In midstream it occurred to me: "Stop this crying, it's false emotion." So I stopped. Then I woke up filled with a deep sense of peace and joy.

3. Use the Following Simple Method of Interpretation.

Here are four steps that may help you to interpret your dreams. We will apply them to the dream we have just recounted.

• *Title*. If your dream were a short story, what title would you give it? When I thought about my dream, I thought I'd call it "The Hug"!

• *Theme*. What is the main gist of the dream, what does it seem to be about?

After reflecting on my encounter with St. Thérèse, I believed it was saying that true love tests all things, while providing the *desire* and the *power* to change.

• *Feeling*. Dreams are mostly about our emotional reactions to internal and external issues. So it is important to ask: "What was the main feeling in my dream; was it fear, joy, relief, guilt, love?" I had many feelings as I dreamt but the principal feeling was one of joy in being loved.

• *Question*. What is the dream trying to bring to my attention? For example, my dream seemed to raise a number of important questions. Firstly, do I accept that spiritual love and physical affection can be reconciled in my life as a priest? Secondly, in the light of love, do I want to change my life in any way? Thirdly, can I abandon guilt feelings of a self-absorbed kind? Finally, as a man, am I at home with the feminine self, and for that matter, with the women I meet?

4. Move from Literal to Metaphorical Interpretation of Dreams.

Some dreams can be interpreted in a literal way. Even when they can, they may also have a metaphorical meaning. More often than not, dreams are about inward states rather than external events. For example, a person might have a vivid and disturbing dream about his or her own death and funeral. Interpreted in a literal way, it might be seen as a sign that the person was going to die soon. Interpreted in a metaphorical way, the dream is seen as a dramatisation of the person's fear of life, and a tendency to retreat from its demands and difficulties. As Artemidorus put it: "To dream of death is good for those in fear, for the dead have no more fears."

5. See the Dream in the Context of Everyday Events

Usually our dreams are inner responses to the conflicts and issues of the recent, or sometimes of the distant, past. So when you have become aware of the main theme and feeling in a dream ask:

> • "When did I feel that way during the past few days?" This may not be an easy question to answer, because we are often unaware of our feelings in the rush of everyday life. That's the very reason that the unconscious represents them in a symbolic way in our dreams. It is gently inviting us to accept and deal with them in a realistic way.

If we do recall a significant incident that may have triggered the dream, we can ask:

> • "What was it about that incident that evoked my feeling of fear, guilt, relief, hostility?"

The answer, may lead to this final question:

> • "Does my dream cast any light on my reaction to situations like the one I have recalled, does it point to a constructive way forward?"

6. Learn to Interpret Symbols.

Symbols are the language of the dream. Feelings, desires, issues and conflicts are all represented in symbolic costumes in the night-time videos of the mind. To learn to interpret dreams, we have to become increasingly sensitive to the subtleties of symbolism. It takes time and experience because the meaning of symbols depends upon the context in which they occur. For example, water can be a symbol of such diverse things as life, death, purification, the unconscious. I have found that two books by Tom Chetwynd are particularly helpful in the interpretation of symbols, *A Dictionary For Dreamers*, and *A Dictionary Of Symbols*. Both are published in paperback by Paladin.

Dreams and the Future

Many people are tempted to see their dreams as predictions of future events. By and large, this kind of mental astrology is unrealistic. However, some dreams can have a predictive element. For example, Carl Jung would sometimes send a client for a medical check-up as a result of listening to his or her dream. Occasionally it would suggest, in symbolic manner, that the dreamer had an as-yet undetected disease such as cancer. Jung felt that because of the intimate link between body and mind, the unconscious could detect the beginnings of disease before there were any symptoms.

It is also possible that a person will have an unconscious intuition about the physical, emotional or spiritual state of another person. An insight like this into a present reality can contain within it the seeds of future possibilities. These intuitions may find a voice in dream symbolism. For example, a woman may intuitively sense that her mother is ill. Then in a dream, she sees her mother die. Months later, the mother does become ill and die.

Finally, there is a more inspired kind of dream about future events. This type is prompted by God for a purpose, for example, the dreams of Joseph in Matthew's gospel. While this kind of dream is possible, it is not very likely. God the Father wants us to leave the future in his hands, and to trust him one day at a time.

Dreams and Discernment

How do we know if a dream is natural or a revelation from God? Well, like any other inspiration, we can examine it from at least four points of view. The scriptures say: "It is God who gives the ability to interpret dreams." (Gen. 40:8) As a result, we pray to the Lord, asking him to give us the grace of discernment. Then we go on to consider these questions:

1. Does the content of the dream tend to move me forward into a deeper relationship with God and the spiritual realm?

2. Does the dream help me to accept myself, to be myself, and to forget myself in outgoing love of God and humanity?

3. Does the dream leave me with an ongoing sense of consolation—joy, peace, hope, gratitude—or does it leave me with an inner sense of desolation—restlessness, morbidity, disturbance? Feelings of consolation usually come from the Holy Spirit, whereas feelings of desolation do not.

4. Does the dream help me in any way to resist temptation and to embrace the will of God with conviction? If I can answer "yes", I have probably experienced the "dark speech of the spirit".

A Gift From God

The ability to dream is a gift from God. It can heal the rift between the conscious and the unconscious mind, between rational and pre-rational forms of experience. Dreaming can help us to grow in self-knowledge and in the knowledge of God. Dreaming can lead us into deep, satisfying forms of personal prayer, when it reveals feelings and issues that can be shared with God in loving communication. Finally, dreaming can help us to discover what we really desire. The Dreamer within fills us with holy longings for the coming of God's Kingdom, longings that will be fulfilled when we wake from the sleep of death, to behold the Lord, no longer as in a glass darkly, but face to face.

5
Christian Friendship

Modern psychology has confirmed the intuitions of great writers like Dante and Shakespeare. Our lives unfold through a sequence of phases. Perhaps no one has contributed more to our understanding of this process than German psychologist Erik Erickson. He says that there are eight stages in life. By the age of twenty we have already completed five of them! In adult life only three remain. Each has its own specific developmental task.

- In early adulthood, between 20 and 40 (approx.), the focus is on loving.
- In middle adulthood, between 45 and 60 (approx.), the emphasis shifts to caring.
- In late adulthood, from 65 onwards (approx.), the challenge is to grow old gracefully.

So the ability to mature as an adult rests on the foundation stone of love. It amounts to a choice between intimacy and isolation. The extent to which intimacy is rejected is the extent to which the ability to care or to grow old gracefully is undermined.

Clearly intimacy is important, But what is it exactly? Is it the kind of union experienced during sexual intercourse? Or is it a sort of comradeship e.g. the sort that can exist between soldiers during wartime?

Could it be the type of warm affection that often unites people, e.g. the members of a religious community? I don't think it is necessarily any of these things. I say this because the word itself comes from the Latin meaning "to publish, to make known that which is inmost". It implies some form of mutual self-revelation. We can feel close to a person without any depth of sharing. As American psychologist, Lillian Rubin has written: "Intimacy is some kind of reciprocal expression of feeling and thought, not out of fear of dependent need, but out of a wish to know another's inner life and to be able to share one's own." In this section we are going to examine Christian friendships as *the* model of adult intimacy.

Friendship in the Scriptures

Friendship in the Old Testament
Friendship is mentioned throughout the Old Testament, but especially in the Wisdom books. Perhaps the most striking verses are to be found in Sir. 6:14-18: "A faithful friend is something beyond price, there is no measuring his worth. A faithful friend is the elixir of life, and those who fear the Lord will find one. Whoever fears the Lord makes true friends, for as a man is, so is his friend".

Other Wisdom texts deal with practical things such as the need for a probationary period, telling friends what you feel, the importance of loyalty and confidentiality, etc. The friendship between David and Jonathan embodies all of these ideals. It is recounted in (1 Sam. chapters 18-20). We are told: "Jonathan became one spirit with David and loved him as himself . . . He swore eternal friendship with David because of his deep affection for him. He took off the robe he was wearing and gave it to David, together with his armour and also his sword, bow and belt." This ideal of shared love and goods was to come to fruition in the life of Jesus and the early Church.

Friendship in the Life of Jesus
Jesus's relationship with the Father was the ruling passion of his life. He interpreted family ties, marriage and friendship in the light of this sense of divine intimacy.

Let's look at each relationship in turn. Firstly, when Jesus left his home in Nazareth, he re-established his relationship to Mary and his relatives.

He said: "Whoever does what God wants him to do is my brother, my sister, my mother." (Mk. 3:35) Secondly, Jesus renounced marriage in favour of celibacy. It's not that he was a prude, or anti-sex. He explained: "In heaven there will be neither marriage nor giving in marriage." (Mt. 22:30) He wanted to be a witness to these ultimate truths. Thirdly, Jesus formed many adult friendships. He was close to Lazarus and his two sisters. He was intimate with the apostles, especially Peter, James, and John, "the beloved disciple". But once again he interpreted these relationships in terms of his union with God. "I have called you friends," he declared, "because I have told you everything I have heard from my Father." (Jn. 15:15)

Clearly, Jesus desired to be intimate with the apostles. He wanted to reveal to them the deepest thoughts and feelings of his heart. But his best efforts ended in frustration. This became quite obvious on the occasion when Philip said: "Show us the Father." With exasperation Jesus replied: "Whoever has seen me has seen the Father, why then do you say, 'show us the Father'?" (Jn. 14:8-12)

The Holy Spirit and Divine Intimacy

A friend desires to be united as fully as possible with the person he loves. He wants to do this by means of mutual self-disclosure. However, the fact that we are separate individuals makes this well–nigh impossible. St. Paul explains why this is so: "It is only a person's own spirit within him that knows all about him." (1 Cor. 2:11) In other words, while I have a direct awareness of myself, I can only have a partial, indirect knowledge of another person. This remains true, no matter how much he tells me about himself.

Needless to say, Jesus had a direct awareness of himself. But as a result of being filled with the Holy Spirit at the time of his baptism, he also had a direct awareness of his Father. There was no barrier between them. Jesus would say: "You, Father are in me, and I in you." (Jn. 17:21) It was precisely this experience of God that Jesus couldn't convey to the apostles. They heard his words. They understood to a certain extent. But they couldn't stand inside his skin. So they couldn't share in his sense of intimacy with the Divine.

Over a period of time Jesus concluded that his words, no matter how eloquent, would not be enough. Only the Holy Spirit would be able to lead the apostles and disciples into the truth about God. As a result, Jesus began to talk in a mysterious and paradoxical way. On one occasion he said: "The Spirit is *with* you now, soon he will be *within* you." (Jn. 14:17) This was both a statement of fact and a promise. It was a fact in the sense that while Jesus was *with* the apostles the Spirit was with them. This was so because Jesus was the Christ i.e. the One who is filled with the Spirit. It was a promise in the sense that Jesus was saying that a time would come when the same Holy Spirit would be poured out on his apostles and disciples. Then it would dwell *within* them and they would have "that mind which was in Christ". (1 Cor. 2:16) Jesus said that he would have to leave his followers before the Spirit could be given to them: "It is better for you that I go away, because if I do not go, the Helper will not come to you. But if I go away, then I will send him to you." (Jn. 16:7) In saying this, Jesus was referring to his forthcoming death and resurrection. They would be the necessary prelude to the sending of the Spirit.

Pentecost and Friendship With Christ

Jesus saw his death as a sacrifice of friendship. "The greatest love a person can have for his friends," he says, "is to give his life." By his death on the cross Jesus would be able to yield up his Spirit to the Lord. Then the Father would pour out the same Spirit on all those who believed in his Son. So the last words that Jesus spoke on the cross: "Into thy hands I commend my Spirit" (Lk. 23:46) were a necessary preparation for Pentecost. On that momentous day the promises were fulfilled. The apostles, together with Mary and the other disciples, were drenched and soaked in the Spirit of God. Their relationship with Jesus was transformed. He was no longer the One who was *with* them. They were consciously aware that he was living *within* their hearts. It is said that after his resurrection Jesus could walk through the walls of a room. Having received the Holy Spirit, the believers felt as if Jesus had walked through the walls of their bodies. They could say with St. Paul: "We no longer live, Christ Jesus lives in us." (Gal. 2:20)

Friendship in the Early Church

In the fifth century B.C. a Greek holy man called Pythagoras founded a community of friends. It had four guidelines.

1. Friends share in the perfect communion of a single spirit.
2. Friends share everything in common.
3. Friends are equals, and friendship is an indication of equality.
4. A friend is a second self.

These ideals, which echo the teaching of the Old Testament, were developed by later Greek writers Plato and Aristotle. It's said that when Aristotle was asked to define friendship, he replied: "One soul dwelling in two bodies." I mention this because, when St. Luke came to describe the early Christian community, he saw it as the fulfilment of these ancient ideals. United by their faith in Jesus, the first believers "were one in heart and soul, and no one said that any of the things he possessed was his own, but they had everything in common." (Acts 4:32) In other words, the first Christians were a community of friends. By sharing their love and their goods they fulfilled the ideals of David and Johathan, as well as the first two guidelines of Pythagoras. In the power of the Holy Spirit they carried out the Lord's command that they love one another as he had loved them, i.e. as friends.

The Nature of Christian Friendship

After my ordination I knew a lot *about* Christ, but I didn't know him in a *personal* way. To me he often seemed distant and unreal. I found it hard to pray or to read the scriptures with interest. I wasn't happy with the situation. I began to have a great desire for an outpouring of the Holy Spirit and a spiritual awakening in my life. For nearly two years I prayed for this grace.

Eventually divine providence led me to an ecumenical meeting in Northern Ireland. I heard an Anglican priest preaching about Jesus as the source of our peace. He spoke with extraordinary eloquence and conviction. His words sent shivers down my spine and brought tears to my eyes. I wanted to know the Lord in the way this man did. I approached him and told him of my desire. We talked a little. Then he read the following words of St. Paul: "I pray that Christ will make his home in your hearts through faith. I pray that you may have your roots and foundations in love, so that you, together with all God's people, may have the power to understand how broad and long, how high and deep is Christ's love—

although it can never be fully known—and so be filled with the very nature of God." (Eph. 3:17-20) These verses jumped alive off the page into my heart. They expressed exactly what I longed for at that point in my life.

It was then that the Anglican priest placed his hands on my head and prayed. Something happened. The Spirit fell upon me. I was flooded with a sense of God's love. Jesus became intensely real. From that moment on he was my most intimate friend, my second self. I could identify with the words of poet Tadh Gaelach O Suilleabhain:

> *The light in my heart, O Saviour, is Thy heart,*
> *the wealth of my heart, Thy heart poured out for me*
> *Seeing that Thy heart, Love, filled with love for me*
> *leave Thy heart in keeping, hooded in mine.*

That was over 17 years ago. Since then I have been trying to deepen my relationship with Christ by means of daily prayer. I have also felt called to form intimate friendships with a few fellow Christians.

In the rest of this section we will look at some of the important ingredients and effects of such relationships. Where it seems appropriate we will quote from classical and Christian writings on the subject.

Ten Ingredients of True Friendship

1. *Equality.* Friends have an affinity, a spontaneous liking for one another. They know that their relationship is based on a sense of equality. It is there to start with. Their love for one another makes any differences to do with education, social status, or wealth, irrelevant. They usually share a commitment to values like truth and fidelity. It is worth noting that over the centuries there has been very little writing about male/female friendships. What little there is has tended to be negative and cautionary in tone. The reason for this was not so much a fear of sexual complications, as an assumption that women were not equal to men. As a result, a man could befriend another man but not a woman.

The advent of women's lib and the recognition of male/female equality could change all that. It is a healthy development. As John Powell has written: "For any individual to actualise his potential as a human being he must have the experience of true and deep friendship with a person of the opposite sex."

2. *Goodwill.* Many writers have pointed out that there are three possible

motives for friendship—advantage, pleasure, and goodwill. Only the third provides a basis for true friendship. Friendships based on advantage are common. This is so, because many people focus on the satisfaction of their own emotional and material needs, rather than the needs of their friends. By and large this kind of self-absorption is unconscious. For example, a man who is insecure may latch on to a mature, caring woman. He forms a dependency relationship in the name of love. He uses his friend to ventilate his thoughts, feelings and hurts. In this way he tries to escape from the burden of his aloneness. But he shows very little interest in the inner life of his friend. His is a love based on need, rather than a sense of need based on love.

Friendships based on pleasure are also common, especially those that are motivated by erotic attraction. Despite repeated declarations of love, such relationships may be founded on the fact that friends satisfy one another's sensual desires.

Genuine friendships are based on goodwill. Psychologist Harry Sullivan put it well when he said: "Love begins when a person feels another person's needs are as important as his own." Psychologist Scott Peck is probably closer to Christian perspective when he writes: "I define love thus; the will to extend one's self for the purpose of nurturing one's own or another's spiritual growth." When this kind of love is the primary dynamic in a relationship, advantages and pleasure may follow as a consequence rather than as a motive for the friendship.

3. *Trust*. The first developmental task we face as children is the ability to trust the people around us, especially our parents. It's a task of crucial importance, because it is the foundation stone upon which the ability to be intimate is based. After all, how could a person reveal his deepest thoughts and feelings if he feared rejection, or betrayal? Cicero anticipated the findings of Erik Erickson when he wrote: "Trust and friendship go together." This kind of trust is evoked by the ongoing awareness of being accepted, liked, respected, appreciated and loved.

4. *Loyalty*. It is an important ingredient of friendship. In the Book of Sirach 6:7 we read: "When you gain a friend test him?" In other words, friendships need a probation period. This delay is needed to ensure that the potential friend has the right qualities and motives for the relationship. If the man or woman in question is suitable, there should be a profession

of friendship, love and loyalty. As Sirach says: "Every friend declares his friendship." (37:1) We have already noted the example of Jonathan in the Old Testament, and that of Jesus in the New Testament. Jonathan's loyalty was such that he was prepared to risk his life for David. Jesus proved his love by laying down his life for his friends. As St. Aelred commented: "There is nothing more praiseworthy in friendship than loyalty, which seems to be its nurse and guardian."

5. *Forgiveness.* Even the best of friends will occasionally hurt one another. This is inevitable because no one is perfect. Whether as a result of weakness or of malice, even friends can say or do things that they later come to regret. Hurts lead to anger. Affection can be overshadowed by bitterness or resentment. The only cure in such circumstances is forgiveness, a humble willingness either to ask for forgiveness for having caused pain, or to freely and willingly forgive a friend who has caused hurt. In this way friendship becomes a school. As friends forgive people they like, they learn to forgive people they don't like.

6. *Respect.* Friends appreciate one another's values. They avoid asking one another to do anything that would offend against conscience. This could be particularly relevant when it comes to the expression of physical affection between men and women, especially those who are not married. In instances like this, the stricter conscience should rule. As Cicero wrote: "So this is the guideline we must lay down between friends, don't do anything that is wrong, and if you are asked for such a thing, turn the application down. To excuse oneself for committing a misdemeanour, on the grounds that it is done for the sake of the friend, is entirely unacceptable."

7. *Communication.* A priest psychologist, Fr. Henri Nowwen, has suggested that there are five degrees of intimacy. They include relationships with:
- Acquaintances e.g. the milkman or postman.
- Colleagues e.g. the girls in a typing pool.
- Relatives e.g. uncles, aunts and cousins.
- Family and friends.
- Intimate friends.

What makes intimate friends different from the other relationships is the depth of mutual self-disclosure involved. All the classical writers, Christian and non-Christian, agree on this. St. Francis de Sales wrote: "Friends love one another. They know they love another. And they have communication, intimacy and familiarity with one another . . . for this is the basis of friendship."

What should be communicated? Cicero gave a general answer: "You can speak as freely as to your own self about any and every subject upon earth." St. Aelred is more specific: "A friend shares *all* the secrets of your innermost heart. You are so closely united to him as to become almost one. To him you confide *everything* as if he were your other self." The phrase, "As if he were your other self", is a key one. In private moments we take off our public masks and uniforms. As we reflect on our deeper experiences, we become aware of our most personal feelings, desires and secret vulnerabilities. In an intimate friendship these are communicated without editing or censorship. This is possible because mutual trust and acceptance create a climate of psychological safety. It encourages increasing levels of honest self-disclousure, in a shared desire to know and be known.

Many men have a problem with this kind of communication. It may be due to the fact that they are out of touch with their feelings or find it hard to name and express them. This has many unfortunate results. Intimate friendship is a good deal less common among men than it is among women. Even when men claim to be best friends, there can be a distinct lack of self disclosure. Their relationships are often based on shared activities and talk about things like sport, politics, work, women and the like. However, deeper personal feelings and problems are not shared.

In contrast, women's friendship are generally based on shared intimacies, self-disclosure, nurturance and emotional support. As a result they can experience disappointment in marriage. Because many men find self-revelation either impossible or extremely difficult, their wives feel lonely and frustrated. Instead of being intimate friends, such couples become "intimate strangers" who share their lives and bodies but not their hearts.

That said, most men have both a need and a capacity for intimate relationships. Research has shown that they are more likely to achieve success with a woman rather than with a man. Unlike male friendships, male/female relationships are less likely to fall victim of the macho stereotypes that imply that all sense of vulnerability has to be hidden by men. The women will usually lead by example. But as Lillian Rubin has written: "What she's asking of the man is a sharing of his inner life and thoughts not out of fear, not out of a need to be cared for, but out of the wish to expose that part of himself." The woman needs to be patient. She has to avoid poking with probing questions into areas that haven't been voluntarily opened up. Needless to say, this cautionary note applies to the man as well!

8. *Listening.* Intimacy among adults is expressed in a wish to know another inner life along with the ability to share one's own. That's why friends really listen to one another. To be specific, they listen with empathy rather than sympathy or apathy. Let me explain.

(a) Listening with apathy. The focus here in on *facts* and *ideas* rather than personal understanding. A woman admits to being anxious, depressed and guilty about excessive eating. The male friend who listens in an apathetic way, asks: "Have you weighed yourself, how much weight have you put on?" When he is given the answer, he replies: "You are eating too much. You should really try to do something about it!" The woman knows this already. But her friend's lack of understanding will reinforce her problem and leave her more likely to continue eating too much.

(b) Listening with sympathy. In this case objectivity is abandoned altogether in order to share in the other person's feelings. For example, the sympathetic listener gets so depressed by the woman's story that he goes with her to the fridge. Together they try to console themselves with "nature's tranquilliser", as food has been called. To share feelings in this way is to become part of the problem. It isn't really helpful.

(c) Listening with empathy. Here the intention is to recognise what the other person feels, and to respond emotionally to those feelings, without having to share them. When the person with empathy hears the woman's story, he might respond: "I felt a real surge of tenderness for you when I sensed how your anxiety and depression had led you to eat more than you wanted." This kind of response helps the woman. She feels accepted and understood. As a result she may feel less inclined to over-eat.

Good listeners avoid talking about themselves. Sometimes what a friend says reminds us of a memory or feeling of our own. Mention of a death may bring to mind a similar death in our family. We may begin to listen to our own emotion filled memory. We say: "I know what you are going through. I went through the same thing two years ago", while going on to recount the details. Instead of listening to the other person, we are in effect, asking him or her, to listen to us. While we may have the best of intentions in sharing like this, it isn't really helpful. It is self-absorbed. In any case, no two people react in the same way to death. Everyone's experience is unique. Dietrich Bonhoeffer once wrote: "Many people are looking for an ear that will listen. They do not find it among Christians because Christians are too busy talking when they should be listening." While this may be true of many relationships, it is not a characteristic of genuine friendships.

9.*Confidentiality*. It is very important in friendships. There is nothing worse than hearing someone recounting a secret that you shared with a friend in confidence. It seriously undermines the trust upon which intimacy depends. As (Sir. 22:21-22) says: "Even if you have a violent argument with a friend, and speak sharply, all is not lost. But any friend will leave you if you reveal his secrets." Echoing this sentiment, St. Aelred said that if a friend betrays a confidence, "It destroys the very foundations of love and pleasantness between friends."

10. *Correction*. All of us are blind to our faults to a certain extent. We see the speck in a brother's eye while failing to see the beam in our own. Because friends love one another and are committed to their mutual growth, they offer and accept correction in a spirit of trust. As John Powell has said: "Love without the truth is sentimentality, while truth without love is cruelty." So friends follow the advice of St. Paul by "speaking the truth in love." (Eph. 4:15)

Some Effects of Christian Friendship

Friendship Increases Happiness

Aristotle went so far as to say: "Without friends, no one would want to live." A few hundred years ago Francis Bacon suggested that, without friendship and self-disclosure, people tend to become "cannibals of their own hearts". But when a person enjoys an intimate friendship it has two main effects—it doubles joys and seems to cut sorrows in half. St. Thomas Aquinas wrote: "Friends delight in each other's presence, enjoy each other's actions and talk and find comfort in their anxieties. Does trouble come? Then straightaway we seek our friend."

Friendship Heals

In adult life most of us are aware of inner hurts. We lack integration. We are bedevilled by neurotic fears and compulsions. Psychologists argue convincingly that many of our adult problems can be traced back to our experience of childhood. Some of these experts maintain that healing can only come through either psychotherapy or psychoanalysis. Both are time-consuming and expensive. Other experts believe that healing can come as a result of experiencing adult love. This is certainly true of intimate friendships. We will look at their therapeutic effects from two points of view—growth in self-esteem and in psychosexual maturity.

Many of us can identify with the story of Dr. Jekyll and Mr. Hyde. Like Stevenson's character we are divided within. We accept those aspects of our character which conform to our beliefs and values. However, we feel that the darker side of our personality is contemptible and unlovable. Because we cannot accept this inept, weak and irrational side of our experience, we conceal the Mr. Hyde within. Honest self-disclosure is avoided as we put on masks and hide behind roles. This may be true of our relationships, but it begins to change in intimate friendships.

The word *friend* comes from the middle-English *frend* and the Anglo-Saxon *freond* which meant "loving", as the present participle of *freogan* meaning "to love". It can also mean "free", because in Anglo-Saxon it referred to the "dearly beloved"members of a household as opposed to the slaves.

When we experience the love of a friend we begin to feel free to take off our masks. We sense a growing urge to give the greatest gift of all, i.e. the gift of our true selves. As this desire strengthens, it begins to override our fear of rejection, a feeling that echoes back to childhood. We begin to lower our defences and to tell our friend about the more vulnerable side of our nature. Weaknesses, fears and sins are revealed. But as we sense the understanding, acceptance and love of our friend a wonderful healing begins to take place. In the light of this friendship-love we begin to understand, accept and love ourselves as we are, and not as we have pretended to be. In this way the enemy within is redeemed. Dr. Jekyll is reconciled by Mr. Hyde. There is a growing sense of inner freedom, and a newfound ability to forgive and love our enemies in the wider community (c.f. Mt. 5:44)

Male/female friendships bring about another kind of healing by helping each person to grow in psycho-sexual maturity. Let me explain. The word *sex* in English comes from the Latin *secare* which means "to cut", i.e. "to divide". The sexes are divided in two inter-related ways. Firstly, men and women are divided from one another by physical and psychological differences. Some of the latter are due to *nature*, others to *nurture*, i.e. the influences of our cultural prejudices and stereotypes. Secondly, men and women are divided within themselves. Carl Jung has suggested that all of us are bi-sexual from a psychological point of view. As a man I am consciously, and predominantly male. But at an unconscious level there is a feminine dimension or *anima,* as Jung called it. Conversely, while women are predominantly and consciously female, at an unconscious level there is a masculine dimension or *animus* to use Jung's term. It is by means of heterosexual intimacy that men and women are reconciled to one another in love and experience an inner reconciliation of the male/female side of their natures.

This point of view accords with church teaching. In Part III of the document *Human Life is Sacred* we read: "Sexuality is one of the most powerful of our biological and emotional endowments. It is one of the deepest constituents of personality. Men and women are complementary to one another, nor just in their physical sexuality, but also in their psychology, their sensitivity and even, in important respects, in their spirituality. The words of Genesis have a profound meaning: "The Lord said, It is not good that the man should be alone. I will make him a helpmate like himself." (Gen. 2:12. Par. 85)

In Ireland there is a magazine for religious called *Intercom.* A few years ago it brought out a controversial edition entitled "In Praise of Women". It was all about priests' friendships with women. In the course of 14 separate personal reflections, nuns, married women and single women shared their experience of friendship with priests and vice-versa. While many of the contributors enjoyed intimacy with members of their own sex they felt that relationships with members of the opposite sex were more satisfying. As the friends came to admire and appreciate specific qualities in one another, they began to become consciously aware of the hidden presence of those same qualities within themselves. For example, one of the priests wrote: "All in all, the closer relationships I have enjoyed with some women have had a humanising effect on me. I have come to realise that the ability to love and be loved is essential for growth towards full humanity. The 'he-man' mystique and the attitude of independent virility, which seem to be expected of me as a man among men, always seem to break down in the company of women. It has been mainly through my relationship with them that I have come first of all to experience and then acknowledge and accept my more tender feelings as part of me, and to recognise my role as an independent he-man as untrue to myself."

No doubt many other men, married and single, could identify with these observations. In another testimony a single woman in her thirties wrote: "In my case the most important aspect of the relationship initially was the feeling of being accepted as a person, and above all a woman. This had a most healing effect on my inner being, as if a gap had been bridged, or a hole mended! I realised that during adolescence and early adulthood I had repressed many feelings because they seemed inappropriate to maturity whereas they were, in fact, just feminine feelings. The understanding and solid male shoulder on which I could now weep, when required, soon sorted out and helped me to accept and thus to cope with my emotions instead of squashing them."

In the statement published at the end of the Synod on the Laity we read: "Women, you justly fight for the full recognition of your dignity and rights. May this struggle give birth to a world of dialogue, a world where man and woman complement each other as willed by the Creator." (par. 13). Surely, there is no better place to begin than in heterosexual friendship!

Friendship Enlightens
Francis Bacon was of the opinion that friends learned more from one another during an hour together than they could through a day spent in private meditation. Besides sharing knowledge, friends can offer one another objective advice and help one another to come to sound judgments and decisions. They also learn about virtues through their exercise in the relationship e.g. patience, kindness, self-control and the like.

Friendship is also a school of love. Shared intimacy progressively releases the friends from their self-absorption, as a result of the inner healing they experience. Consequently, they are more disposed to love people in general. Commenting on the relationship of Dante and Beatrice, Joseph Pieper writes: "If we look to well-documented experience of great loves, we learn that precisely this intensity of love turned toward a single partner seems to place the lover at the vantage point from which he realises for the first time the goodness and lovableness of *all* people."

Genuine friendships are particular but not exclusive. By loving one another, friends learn to love even in the least of the brethren the Christ they have first come to recognise in themselves.

Friendship Leads to God

Scripture teaches that God lives in each of us. In an earlier section entitled *Pentecost and Friendship with Christ* we saw how this truth is experienced by the power of the Holy Spirit. As the dynamic of love draws friends closer together through sharing, they come closer to the God in whom they live and move and have their being. (c.f. Acts 17:28) As they offer one another the gift of love and acceptance, they become for one another icons or parables of the presence of Jesus. As this awareness penetrates, each friend gets in touch with his or her deeper self, rooted as it is in the love of God. As the friends share the gift of their love in this committed way, there may be ecstatic moments when their separateness gives way to a union of their personalities in the awareness of God. In this way the friends, united as they are in mind and heart, come to experience for themselves the truth of Jesus's words: "Where two of three come together in my name, there am I with them." (Mt. 18:20) In his book, *Spiritual Friendship*, St. Aelred of Rievaulx has written: "God is friendship." It does sound strange, doesn't it? And there is no authority for it in scripture. But I wouldn't hesitate to attribute to friendship anything associated with charity, as for instance, "He who abides in friendship abides in God, and God abides in him." St. Francis de Sales wrote: "Friendship is excellent because it comes from God. Excellent because its very bond is God. Excellent because it will last eternally in God."

Friendship Teaches Us to Pray

In the Old Testament prayer was seen as a friendship with God. In

Exodus we read about the way in which Moses conversed with the Lord. He would enter the tent of meeting i.e. the place of relationship. There he would be overshadowed by the cloud of the divine presence i.e. the Holy Spirit. Then "Yahweh would speak with Moses face to face as a man does with his friend." (Ex. 33:11) St Teresa of Avila echoes this experience when she describes prayer in these famous words: "Prayer is nothing other than intimate friendship, a frequent heart to heart conversation, with Him by whom we know ourselves to be loved." So the dynamics of prayer are the same as those involved in any intimate friendship, a matter of heartfelt self-disclosure to God and loving attention to his revelation of Himself.

Because we know that Jesus is our dearest friend we disclose all our innermost secrets to Him. Why share such things with the Lord? Doesn't He know them anyway? True, but he wants us to reveal our real selves to Him, not because He needs it, but because He knows we do. There are three main reasons for this.

• The impulse of love is to give. The greatest gift we can give the Lord is the gift of our true selves.
• We will never feel that we are truly loved and accepted by the Lord until we know he loves and accepts us as we are.
• This kind of honesty opens the heart to revelation. The extent to which we hide our experiences from Jesus is the extent to which we will be closed to his inspirations.

So in personal prayer we go beyond facts and ideas to share our deeper feelings and experiences. We tell God about our reactions to Himself. For example we may feel angry because we think that he has failed to answer our prayers for a sick relative. We tell him about our reactions to daily events, e.g. joy on receiving a proposal of marriage, or distress as a result of seeing pictures of famine victims on TV. We can even talk to God about our feelings in relation to ourselves e.g. guilt on account of unloving behaviour and the like.

Usually, it's not too difficult to share our positive feelings with the Lord. The trouble arises when we try to come to him, not in our Sunday best, but in the ragged clothes of our anger, fear and guilt. Some people try to repress feelings like these as wrong or inappropriate. When they are buried alive in this way, they can turn into numbing states of anxiety and depression. Prayer becomes formal. We may continue to go through the motions, but the Lord seems distant and unreal. Other people avoid repressing their feelings. Instead they are honest *with themselves* in the Presence of God, rather than being honest *to the God* who is present. We only pray in an intimate way when we express *all* our feelings, positive and negative, to the Lord, without censorship or editing.

I need hardly say that the Lord wants to reveal himself, especially to his friends. As our desire to know Him is expressed in loving attention to all aspects of reality, God manifests Himself. We become aware of Him as "The Beyond in the midst of our lives". For example, we may be focusing on a gospel scene when all of a sudden Jesus becomes palpably real to us. I can recall a recent retreat when the memory of an incident in the life of Jesus kept on bringing tears of joy to my eyes. I became so aware of his love for me, that my heart "burned within". (Lk. 24:32)

God can reveal Himself through other people. As the poet Hopkins wrote: "Christ plays in ten thousand places, lovely in limbs and lovely in eyes not His, to the Father, through the features of men's faces." When we pay attention to what people say about their relationship to God it can be very inspiring. Through their story, we may enter into a new awareness of the presence and word of God ourselves.

The Lord can be revealed through nature. A hymn in the Divine Office says: "The Father gave his children the wonder of the world, in which his power and glory like banners are unfurled." Speaking of poor Irish farmers, Patrick Kavanagh wrote:

> *Yet sometimes when the sun comes through a gap*
> *These men know God the Father in a tree:*
> *The Holy Spirit is the rising sap*
> *And Christ will be the green leaves that will come*
> *At Easter from the sealed and guarded tomb.*

Art of all kinds can be a means of revelation by God. Milton described how listening to church music affected him:

> *Let the pealing organ blow . . .*
> *As may with sweetness, through mine ear, dissolve me into*
> *ecstasies and bring all heaven before mine eyes.*

So in these and in many other ways the Lord reveals Himself to us. In doing so he brings to light the false images of God that inhabit the pantheon of our minds, e.g. images of God as demanding, vindictive or harsh. As we begin to appreciate what God is really like, we have a grace-prompted desire to express our response in some form of appropriate action. In this way, our Christian action becomes the expression of our friendship with God, instead of being a substitute for it.

Love Transforms

For me, the great beauty of the coming of Jesus lies in the fact that Divine Love found a human face. It is my belief that the Church, the Body of Christ, should show how all that is truly human can be transformed by love. Friendships do this in a lovely and attractive way. Because they teach us to love, they prepare us to care for others with compassion and to grow old gracefully. Like yeast in the bread, they act as a leaven of grace in the wider community.

Some Christians have had the mistaken belief that friendships should be renounced in favour of charity. For example, Danish writer Soren Kierkegaard has written: "The true lover regards the very requirement of reciprocity to be a contamination, a devaluation, and loving without the reward of reciprocated love to be the highest blessedness." To oppose friendship and Christian charity in this way is misguided and unnecessary. St Augustine was correct when he wrote: "There can be no true friendship unless those who cling to each other are welded together by God in that love which is spread throughout our hearts by the Holy Spirit which is given to us."

Friendship is not an end in itself. It is a relationship that comes to fruition through charity, and reaches without destroying itself to the source of all charity, namely God Himself. In doing this the preferential aspect of friendship-love is reconciled to the unconditional nature of charity. We conclude with some beautiful words of St. Aelred: "Friendship is the true glory of the rich, it is home to the exile, money to the poor, medicine to the sick, life to the dead, beauty to the strong, power to the weak, reward to the toiler . . . To crown all this, friendship is a means of perfection, is indeed only a degree short of perfection for from being a friend of man one becomes a friend of God."